Chinese Drama and Society

Chinese Drama and Society

Teresa Chi-Ching Sun

Hamilton Books
Lanham • Boulder • New York • Toronto • London

Published by Hamilton Books
An imprint of The Rowman & Littlefield Publishing Group, Inc.
4501 Forbes Boulevard, Suite 200, Lanham, Maryland 20706
Hamilton Books Acquisitions Department (301) 459-3366

6 Tinworth Street, London SE11 5AL

Copyright © 2019 by The Rowman & Littlefield Publishing Group, Inc.

All rights reserved. No part of this book may be produced in any form or by any electronic means, including information storage and retrieval systems,without written permission from the publisher, except by a reviewer who may quote passages in a review.

British Library Cataloguing in Publication Information Available

Library of Congress Control Number Available:

ISBN 978-0-7618-7131-6 (pbk)
ISBN 978-0-7618-7132-3 (electronic)

Contents

Acknowledgments	vii
Introduction	1

Part I: On Classical Drama

1	A Case Study of Ming Drama: *The Tale of the Lute (琵琶記)*	7
2	The Social and Cultural Characteristics of Chinese Drama	13

Part II: On Drama, East and West

3	The Coming of Western Drama	33
4	The Dispute over Stage Plays and Traditional Chinese Drama: Tragedy and Comedy	49
5	The Movement toward a National Theatre: Renovation and Survival of the Beijing Opera	65
6	Some Thoughts after the Show of *Peony Pavilion*	81
7	Chinese Comic Literature: Discussion of A Witty Short Story	87

Bibliography	99
Index	101
About the Author	105

Acknowledgments

To introduce Chinese cultural activities for study in the United States in the early 1970s was a difficult pioneering task when the Cold War era's frozen relationship between U.S. and China was still firmly set. There was no alternative but to handle it with a cautious yet combative spirit. Besides art and acupuncture demonstrations, a Chinese Beijing opera for the first time ever was performed on a college campus. The cheer echoed among the Chinese community was not only for the appreciation of a dramatic show, but for the fact that Beijing opera was able to enter the grand hall of American higher educational institutions just as the cultural production of any other civilization did. The support of Department of Foreign Language and Literature at California State University, Los Angeles for these activities is really appreciated. Whittier College was also the first few colleges to offer Chinese literature courses in the 1990s, which gave me the opportunity to add the study of drama to my teaching. Thanks for their support too. Li San Bao, the Chair of Asian and Asian American Studies at California State University at Long Beach, asked me to join the faculty in 2000 and I was able to formally teach a course on Chinese drama. A graduate student wrote a thesis on women's issues in Guan Han Qin's drama, again a pioneering effort. A production of *A Taste of Chinese Opera* was successfully performed at the Norris Theater in Palos Verdes Peninsula, the first ever performance at a prestigious Community Theater. The support of the founders of the Norris Theatre, Joan and Dick Moe, deserve gratitude from the Asian American community in South Bay, Southern California. These experiences stimulated my writing of this book. Personally, my husband and family always stood by me while I was trying to promote Chinese culture and the understanding of Chinese people. Last but not least, thanks to my editor, Molly Desjardins.

Introduction

Once a civilization has reached a state of intellectual stasis and satisfaction with its own resolutions to the problems of the universe, it tends to be so self-content that its creative world gradually stagnates. This was the case when China met the West at the turn of eighteenth century. Unfortunately, it was also a time when the Chinese found that their technology was terribly lacking. This allowed for extensive colonization to take place. The West greatly impacted all of Asia, igniting tremendous changes in all areas of Chinese life. It started becoming clear to the Chinese that there were all kinds of people from many civilizations other than what China had ever imaged. Despite awareness of the cultural differences in social customs, religious beliefs, and moral standards, the sparks of intellectual activity in the mindset of the Chinese people helped to expand the horizons of China. Concepts that were previously never thought of were taking over the minds of the people.

The Chinese have long been known for forming their own basic attitudes and values and closely following their prolonged previous traditions. When China was exposed to new ideas and beliefs from the West, the old ways of life were washed over by modernization. Having gone through a swift and diligent exploration of the West, China benefited from adapting aspects of the Western character and its creative world was moving again. The intellectual exchange between civilizations melted the ice wall of solitude that China had built around itself; China's isolationist stance towards international communication was slowly changing.

However, when two very different cultures with limited previous exposure come together they often sharply collide. A clear example of this collision appears at the turn of the century with the introduction of Western drama and novels, which brought to China a new genre of Western-styled stage plays. The style of these new plays, which freed drama from the restrictive norms of traditional Beijing opera, fed into a movement to renovate Chinese opera. But the initial culture shock brought upon more social perplexity than excitement. With the introduction of the Western theory of drama, the new stage drama style was developed and flourished, but the development also aroused a group of Western educated Chinese scholars to publish academic articles attacking the existing style of the Beijing opera. The sharp criticism of existing drama, which was based on a superbly crafted foreign drama style, stirred up patriotic self-awareness among Chinese intellectuals who used the momentum of the new style to help achieve the reform of Chinese opera. A national theater movement sprung up and led to the rejuvenation of Beijing opera in the early Republican era. The performing arts had never before been the topic of such heated discussion. Not only did dramatic elements like plot and acting receive keen attention, but so too did larger questions about performance theory and aesthetic value. Impressed by the literary style and philosophical concepts behind Western drama, progressive Chinese intellectuals whole-heartedly welcomed the literary and dramatic style of the West but intentionally aimed at the social reform of China. The evolution of modern, literary stage drama was an important aspect of the Chinese intellectual movement, transforming stage shows into messengers of social change during the first half of the twentieth century.

The resulting dispute between traditional Chinese opera and its modern, European-countered drama was deemed so fascinating that it is truly worthwhile to conduct a study to reveal and critique the cultural exchange. While there have been productive studies comparing the characteristics of Eastern versus Western theatre, there has not yet been a study examining the social environments that brought these characteristics about.

The meeting of the two cultures in drama raises many questions and this book will discuss them accordingly. If the cause of the theatrical dispute is to be made fully comprehensible for the reader, there needs to be a presentation of both traditional and modern stage drama. Therefore, this study provides knowledge of both in two parts. Part One will present *The Tale of the Lute* (琵琶記), written in the Ming Era, as a case study for the base line of comprehension of classical drama; the piece is far too prominent to not be included. The Ming Empire (1368–1644 AD) was built in a society that was the most isolated from Western influence. Knowing the significance of *The Tale of Lute* (琵琶記) and its cultural backdrop will serve as a reference point for those who wish to understand traditional Chinese drama. This piece of drama best exemplifies the characteristics of a popular classical production. There will be no attempts to apply Western theories to the discussion of *The Tale of Lute* (琵琶記). Discussions on the ethical values portrayed by characters from hundreds of years ago will be presented. Readers should approach this play with its original audience in mind, viewing and appreciating its original Chinese scheme through the eyes of those belonging to viewers from ancient Chinese culture. To prepare readers for the understanding of classic Chinese drama, a briefing of the social background and cultural reasons are presented in chapter 2.

Part Two of the book will switch focus, first addressing the coming of Western drama and the rise of the Chinese stage plays in the early twentieth century. These plays reflect how the many characteristics of Western civilizations were being surprisingly absorbed by Chinese culture. Since many activities and presentations involve this new form of theatre, there will be some discussion on the roles of the new stage drama and its impact on Chinese social movements.

The entrance of Western stage drama in China and how it was initially received by Chinese intellectuals will illustrate the confrontation between the two cultural traditions. The eagerness for social reform among the young Chinese will be suggested as a possible reason for why Western plays, so strange and different, even entered China. Motivated by their impression of Western traditions, Western educated students' overly enthusiastic effort to apply foreign dramatic concepts as a criticism of traditional Chinese theatre will be explained throughout the chapters of Part Two. A particular focus will be given to the reactionary urge amongst Chinese intellectuals toward dramatists who had returned from the West and brought about the sociopolitical debate over Chinese drama. In response to Western challenges, a movement to reform Beijing opera took place. One example of this reform was the elimination of coarse and vulgar expressions in plays, which helped to elevate the social status of Chinese theatrical arts, appealing to the social movements that were happening at the time.

A short chapter on the transformation of a traditional Chinese drama, *Peony Pavilion* (牡丹亭), into a fascinating modern version is added to demonstrate how a classical Kun drama can be converted into a modern operatic stage show with original singing and in a modernized stage show style. Rather than being subordinated, the essence of the Chinese cultural spirit is more expressively conveyed. There have been numerous studies on the style of traditional operatic theatre, called Kun drama in English, but no major studies exist that deal with the rise of the modern stage play and its contextual relationship with the transformation of traditional Kun opera.

One last chapter will be on a piece of comic literature devoted to explaining the kind of comical sentiment that the Chinese would appreciate, since Western-style comedy has not shaped drama in literary China. The story, at its heart, has to do with an intriguing narrative about how a district Magistrate maneuvered with wisdom in defense of the marriage of three young couples and against conventional Confucian ethical judgement.

Part I

On Classical Drama

Chapter One

A Case Study of Ming Drama

The Tale of the Lute (琵琶記)

A BRIEF SUMMARY OF *THE TALE OF THE LUTE* (琵芭記)

In this popular drama from the Ming period, Cai Yong (蔡邕), a poor country boy, is recommended by the district's magistrate and persuaded by his father to take the imperial examination. Married only two months to Zhao Wu Niang (趙五娘), Cai Yong (蔡邕) leaves for the capital with much concealed in his mind because he knows that his aged parents are in need of special care. He passes the examination with highest honors. This attracts the attention of the then prime minister, Niu Seng-ru (牛僧儒). Knowing the potential of Cai Yong's political future, Premier Niu ignores Cai's plea to return home and instead insists that Cai ask for his daughter's hand in marriage. To please Prime Minister Niu, the emperor decrees that the marriage take place. Not content with his prosperous life in the Niu household, Cai Yong attempts unsuccessfully to contact his family back home. At the same time, back in the country village, the devoted Wu Niang completely loses contact with her husband and goes through all kinds of hardships to care for Cai Yong's parents. After the parents die of hunger and disease, Wu Niang buries them with the family's minimal savings and starts a trip to the capital to look for her husband. Disguised as a Taoist nun, she carried the portraits of her mother and father-in-law. Moved by Cai's grave mood of longing to reunite with his family, the Niu daughter eventually gets permission from the Premier to accompany her husband Cai home. One day, as Wu Niang was approaching the capital, she unexpectedly passes by the Mi Tuo Temple (彌陀寺) where a monastery festivity is in procession. She then plays a lute among the crowd, begging for money with the parents' portraits displayed for blessing. Surprised by a sudden visit from a high official of the temple, Wu Niang is hustled out of the Temple's main hall. In haste, she does not take the portraits with her and finds that they have disappeared upon her return. As she is later told, it was the official who took the portraits. Surprised to learn the whereabouts of the portraits, she then goes to the Niu household looking for her husband but pretending to beg for religious compassion. At the door, she is received by Premier Niu's daughter with great sympathy and pity. At the Niu's residence, before reuniting with her husband, she enters the study room of Cai Yong and sees the lost portraits. With much gravity, she writes a poem recalling her hardship and the death of the elders. The reunion between Cai and his first wife, which took place happily, is followed by a trip to pay homage to the graveside of the parents back home. Upon returning to the capital with both wives accompanying him, Cai receives a promotion because of his piety and his marriage settlement. When his father in law, Prime Minister Niu, learns of Wu Niang's caring for the parents, he requests the imperial court to grand both Wu Niang and his daughter royal titles in recognition of their great virtues.

THE AUTHOR

The Tale of the Lute (琵琶記) was the first and best Southern drama (南曲) to overwhelm the stage of the early Ming. The author, Gao Ze Cheng (高則誠) from Wenzhou (溫州), also named Gao Ming (高明), was such an excellent rhetorician and literary composer that the Emperor Ming Tai Zu (明太祖) commended his play by saying that although every household should consume the Four Books and Five Classics[1] as daily necessities, The Tale of the Lute (琵琶記), is needed like a gourmet dish—a special enjoyment for elites and royals. What an honor to have this said about his literary accomplishment.

The unique sociopolitical involvement of Chinese literati is a decisive factor in the development of Chinese drama. The scheme and theme of dramas are not fictions or fantasized tales, but realistic life stories reflecting social and intellectual trends of their time. Gao's life story provides Western readers with a sketch of how a traditional intellectual in Ming China incorporated the revival of Confucianism in his work. The exact dates of Gao's life were not recorded clearly, but a life span from 1304–1370 AD is probably the most accurate. He lived in a time during the downfall of the Yuan (1277–1367 AD) and the beginning of the Ming Dynasty (1386–1644 AD). He was born and raised in a well-to-do elite family full of poets (his grandfather, uncle, cousins, and brother). Talented with a literary mind, he won the title of genius in the local community at a young age. Even though his father died early, he was groomed to be an intellectual and enjoyed a comfortable lifestyle throughout his youth.

Until the end of Yuan period, for the purpose of saving the falling empire, the ruling Mongol government committed itself to enticing the oppressed Han Chinese to reinstate the Civil Examination System, which was resumed in 1314. This conciliatory polity opened the door to young educated Han people to enter the path of sociopolitical mobilization. Benefited by this official act, Gao successfully passed two levels of the examination in 1344 and 1345 and was appointed to the position as district sheriff (彔事) of Chu Zhou (處州).

During his tenure, he was respected and beloved by the people. It was said that he was well versed in the Tao (the Confucian Way) and devoted to caring for people. A stone tablet was erected commemorating his administration. Upon transferring to another post, the magistrate of the prefecture led a group of students to persuade him to stay and honored him to teach for a period. Not long afterwards, he was asked to be the secretary of the Hang Zhou district (杭州行省丞相). His judicious and efficient style in administering the office won him a great reputation again.

As a member of famed literati at the end of the Yuan period, Gao's deep sympathy for the oppressed poor under the Mongolian rulers and laments over the patriot heroes of the late Song dynasty were fully expressed in his poetry. A conflict of emotion between devotion to secular officialdom and to the life of a nature-loving Taoist hermit was constantly the making of his life. In his poetry, longing for the privacy of retirement and for the integrity of political office were both implied. Optimistic about life, yet pessimistically seeking escape to the immortal realm are wishes equally expressed. He usually grappled with these sentiments in poetry by way of scenery presented with splendid serenity. After his retirement from office, he was just as sincerely devoted to the writing of Southern Melody drama (南曲) as he had been to his official life. It is recorded that he was so passionate about *The Tale of the Lute* (琵琶記) that he had locked himself in a tower in desperation to finish the play. It was said that a hole was pounded open on the floor because he was contemplating the rhythm while composing the music.

THE TALE OF THE LUTE (琵琶記) AND ITS SOCIOPOLITICAL BACKGROUND

The Origin of the Story and the Transformation of the Play

Most of the major Chinese dramas have undergone a process of transformation, from simple folk tales to more structured and complicated narratives on stage. *The Tale of the Lute* (琵琶記) was no exception. Before its final version was settled in the Ming period and presented on stage, several versions of the plot had existed in popular forms such as various folk tales and street ballads. Among them, the popular folk tale, *The Virtuous Lady Zhao and the Cai Er Long* (赵贞女蔡二郎) was the most beloved version before the Ming *The Tale of the Lute* in which Cai was portrayed an ungrateful official unwilling to recognize his relation with Lady Zhao. Worse yet, he made his horse kick his wife to death. At that very moment, Cai's sinful behavior angered the God of Heaven. A lightning attack with five thunders was sent and Cai was executed. People often quoted the play for praising the piety of the devoted Lady Zhao and faulting the betrayer Cai Er Lang. Two other dramas, *Cai Bo-jie* (蔡伯喈) and an early Southern drama, *The Top Candidate Zhang Xie* (張協狀元), were all similar versions with a sad ending. In reality, the central focus of all the tales was the life story of Cai Yong (蔡邕), also named Cai Bo-jie (蔡伯喈), who was a famous official of the Eastern Han period. The various versions with sad endings were so popularly performed all over China that when Gao Ming's final version with a happy ending was produced, research interest was aroused.

The thirteenth century Mongolian Empire shocked Europe and left an impression of "brutal barbarian"-style invasion. At the Far East end of the empire, the military regime had a short-lived Yuan Dynasty and never achieved a thorough occupation in China. Besides military strength, the empire showed no sign of cultural superiority. The semantics of the Chinese language were too difficult for the Mongolians, so conquering the minds of the Chinese was never completed as it was with the Manchurian Qing Dynasty. However, the core of Han Chinese cultural traditions were submerged and practiced in full only by the lowest classes and in the South. Loving to be entertained, the Mongols sought a hasty understanding of the Han society through the performing arts and, thus, nourished the development of Chinese drama. When Chinese intellectuals applied their inherited literary ability to creating sophisticated lyrics, style, and music, the splendor of Yuan drama surged. As the Mongol occupation gradually faded away, Ming China, a Chinese state that towered for three hundred years and was comparable to that of the long-lived Han and Tang Empires, was established. To reinstate the Confucian tradition was as vital an official policy as the setting up of the Ming administrative system. Different from the orthodox Confucian Han period (206BC–220AD), the Buddhist-dominated Tang (618–907AD), or the cultural and artistic flourishing of the Song (960–1279AD), the Ming period was governed powerfully by Neo-Confucianism, whose revival movement claimed not only an intellectual foundation for the Chinese state, but also offered firm ethical rules that penetrated deeply into people's daily life. To be recommended as a play for every household during this period suggests that the revision of the play's ending must have answered the call of the authority. A well-written drama must have a happy ending that echoed the positive upright spirit of the rising Ming Empire and the Confucian outlook of life. Consequently, Cai Yong in *The Tale of the Lute* was portrayed differently than he had been in the many previous folk tales, *The Virtuous Lady Zhao and the Cai Er Long* (赵贞女蔡二郎) and *Cai Bo-jie* (蔡伯喈), and *The Top Candidate Zhang Xie* (張協狀元). Instead of being a disloyal husband, as he was in early versions, Cai was now presented as a virtuous official who was reunited with his wife and enjoyed prestige and wealth.

Achieving a place as the most prominent drama in China of its time signaled a parallel between the rising of the Ming Chinese empire and the recurrence of the Confucian ideology.

In favor of the officially designated ideology, issues pertinent to the content of *The Tale of the Lute* (琵琶記) epitomized all the characters of Confucianism. Of humble origin and a self-taught scholar, Cai rose from poverty to officialdom with diligence. He was filial to his parents and was separated from family against his will. His homeward trip devoted to his family was interrupted by powerful people at the capital because of his outstanding achievement in passing the Civil Examination. But Cai could not allow himself to retreat to new comforts. His integrity reminded him of the wellbeing of his family and eventually love and righteousness take charge, leading him to be reunited with his wife, Wu Niang. Suffering and the endurance of hardship forced upon Wu Niang demonstrate the virtues of being a pious daughter-in-law to Cai's parents. One would not be questioning the fairness of women's status at home if one lived in Ming society, where demand for women's chastity and caregiver duties after marriage were particularly emphasized. The distressed Wu Niang had to suffer to earn virtue, which testified to Confucian values. Cai's sacrifice was aimed at fulfilling the ultimate happiness according to the Confucian system—family reunion and official promotion. Cai eventually held a high position and had both his wives living in the same household with him. His endurance of hardship was properly rewarded—Confucian style. It is necessary to add a few lines on what are the so-called "happy endings" of Chinese drama. A large portion of dramas and short stories lead to two major kinds of happy ending: to achieve scholarship by passing the civil examination for official recognition, and to enjoy a "Big Reunion" (大團圓) of family members.

Of the hundreds of classic dramas that have been produced by dramatists since the Yuan period (1277–1367 AD), the ones that enjoyed an everlasting fame in China since their debut are still frequently performed all over China and in all kinds of dramatic styles, such as Kun drama or Beijing opera. But those that have reached a non-Chinese audience outside China are only a few. The so-called five most grand and profound master works have all been translated to English and other languages. Literary discussions on these works are also carried out heartedly among Western scholars. *The Romance of the West Chamber* (西廂記) and *The Romance of the Eternal Palace* (長生殿) are so well known to every household in China that their popularity is similar to what *Romeo and Juliet* or *Hamlet* hold in the Western world. *The Peach Fan* (桃花扇) has lured the attention of Western scholars for a long time with its fascinating love affairs and beautiful Kunqu (昆曲) performance. The recent presentation of *Peony Pavilion* (牡丹亭) in a restyled modern Kunqu (昆曲) version astonished the audience both in China and in the West.[2] Translated by Dr. Jean Mulligan into English in 1980, *Pi Ba Ji, or The Tale of the Lute* (琵琶記), represents another category of drama. Unlike the other four master works, there is no romance between a beauty and a scion of an elite family. A love duet at the center of the drama was a marvel in the theatrical world of the Ming era and remains so today. But without a line of love sayings, *The Tale of the Lute* (琵琶記) has aroused high emotions since the early Ming and has overwhelmingly won the heart of Chinese people for centuries. Though it has attracted much less attention in comparison with the other four "master dramas" mentioned above in the West, it is still popularly performed in China as one of the major Beijing operas. The uniqueness of the Chinese literati's socially conscientious traditions, which affected the worldly outlook of the Chinese people and their emotion in appreciating *The Tale of the Lute*, (琵琶記) must be the reason. There is no need to explain why and how it failed to demonstrate the same radiance for the Westerners today, but why it is still favored by modern day Chinese audiences deserves to be mentioned. The following section will suggest that the drama continues to be relevant because, in addition to its historical origin in riding the tide of the resurrected Confucian ideology of the Ming era, it also represents an important category of plays about ethical life. After a creative period during the Yuan period, drama inherited a rich production style and many were settled in that regulated format during the Ming period, extending to the Empire of the Qing.

NOTES

1. The Four Books: The Great Learning, The Doctrine of the Mean, The Analects, and The Book of Mencius. The Five Classics: The Confucian canon, comprised of The Book of Change, The Book of Odes, The Book of History, The Book of Rites, and The Spring and Autumn Annals.

2. Bai, Xian Yong, (白先勇), 白先勇说昆曲, Modern Version Peony Pavilions (青春版牡丹亭), Lian Jing Publishing Company (聯經出版事業股份有限公司), Taiwan, 2004.

Chapter Two

The Social and Cultural Characteristics of Chinese Drama

CULTURAL SOURCE OF EPISODES

It could be because of the nourishment of the Yellow River plateau that Chinese civilization rewards an earth-bound practical lifestyle, solemn and dignified. With the prophecy of the "Tao of Heaven," the Confucian school has predominately provided ethical and moral rules to govern the Chinese from an early age. Of the three major systems of thought in China, Confucianism, Taoism, and Buddhism, Confucianism is the judgmental authority for human behavior. In the world of Chinese drama, both Buddhism and Confucianism are represented largely on the level of popular teachings, e.g. reincarnation, compassion, and filial piety. Logical argumentation about human existence in relation to the supernatural being, God, and nature has not been emphasized. Though Taoism clearly presents a metaphysical world, the Natural Tao, Chinese drama has focused primarily on the folk Taoist religion.

In a society like the Ming where ethical law was mainly derived from Confucian doctrine, Taoist thought, and Buddhist teachings, drama episodes mainly dealt with the wisdom of these schools of thought. Moral teaching addressed in these tales is mainly within this framework and is not in the form of sophisticated philosophical inquiry. Ethical laws and religious beliefs are usually delivered directly. The codes of Confucian ethics are centered on kinship living. Family-centered virtues, the Four Ethical Principles, and the Eight Cardinal Virtues (四維八德)[1] have been the essential topics of these dramas. Historical tales of filial piety, chasteness, loyalty, and righteousness are the virtues cherished. Therefore, in addition to the Confucian ethics illustrated in *The Tale of the Lute* (琵琶記), the executing of oppressors and the corrupted for justice are also overwhelmingly dramatized in these tales. For example, the *Orphan Zhao* (趙氏孤兒) by an anonymous author, *Loyalty* (精忠記) by Yao Mao-liang (姚茂良), and *Heroic Tales from the Water Margin* (水滸傳) are all popular dramas, not love tales. They were favored dramas transmitting ethics and the resonance of these messages was tremendously powerful.

From the Taoist school, tales largely remain in a popular sphere. The Yin/Yang and five elements (陰陽五行), immortality, the magic powers of Taoist gods and goddesses, and fortune telling have all joined to contribute to a moral message. *Merry Go Lucky* (風花雪月) by Wu Chang-ling (吳昌齡), *Golden Young Couple* (金童玉女) by Jia Zong-ming (賈仲明), and *San Yuan Ji* (三元記) by Shen Shou-xian (沈受先) are all the best dramas which not only tell the story of Taoist religion but are also amazingly mixed with Buddhist teachings.

Down to the Yuan and Ming eras, Buddhist teachings had already saturated the daily life of Chinese people. Reincarnation, the automatic repayment of good deeds in later life, predestinated fate, and the demonstration of magic powers by Buddhist gods had all been fictionalized and illustrated in drama. As another major source for the writing of drama and novels, Buddhist teaching often transformed into Confucianism-based thought. Hardship and good deeds had to be rewarded and evil behavior and desires had to be punished. Historical events or legends were often fictionalized, such as in *The Journey to the West* (西遊記) by Wu Cheng-en (吳承恩) and *The Tang Tripitaka's Journey Seeking Sutras to the West* (唐三藏西天取經) by Wu Chang-ling (吳昌齡), and *The Bodhisattva Subjugates the Ocean Demon* (泗州大怪淹水母) by Xu Zi-shou (須子壽).

THEATRE AND RESPONSIBILITY FOR PUBLIC EDUCATION

The Chinese theatre that has flourished since the Yuan time has mainly catered to the less educated and satisfied the need of the great masses to be entertained. Dominated by farm living, most commoners did not read and write. To conquer the difficulty of learning the classics and acquiring a philosophical understanding of social issues and human nature was not expected from the audience of the Chinese theater. Therefore, episodes of drama usually were treated realistically and from an earthly perspective, with events strung together one after another. Moral messages were straightforwardly given and directly delivered in the conclusion without any philosophical or psychological notes. The leading roles, heroes or heroines, usually demonstrated virtuous behavior or articulated a religious message. The audience of a common household would be entertained as well as educated by these tales. Thus, the theatrical performance on stage, like the Song storyteller's oral recitals, actually took charge of transmitting knowledge of national traditions and moral teachings among the commoners. They carried a great deal of responsibility for public education.

This kind of social responsibility entrusted to the performing arts is not emphasized in the Western world. Inherited from these traditions, even the modern-day new stage drama still carries out this practical function on stage, except that moral message oftentimes has been replaced by the promotion of social reform.

In view of what has been discussed above, it is undeniable that the difference in approach of Western and Chinese drama represents one of many expressions of the basic difference between the two civilizations. The stagecraft of Chinese drama and plots of short stories shaped by Chinese social and cultural values are quite different from the drama of the West. Wealth, royalty, and love are not direct attractions in life for the Chinese. In Chinese drama, wealth will come as reward of passing the civil examination and gaining public appointment. Royalty is unreachable, and love between a man and a woman is not singled out to be cherished as a great passion.

SOCIAL STATUS

For thousands of years, the Confucian elite-gentry class has been the pillar of the Chinese society. They merged to manage the country as guardians of China's moral tradition and as public administrators. By way of this status, they shouldered the responsibility of both "church and state" in the West combined. The official approval of their public and social status was the endorsement of the civil examination through which they had to distinguish themselves by their literary accomplishments and learning of the classics. The different privileges and degree of prestige as designated by the examination has been so firmly recognized that a man like Cai, who passed the examination with a high score, would be treated royally. It could be said that the entire history of classic novels and dramas centers around the civil examination. Numerous dramatic stories start with a young scholar's trip to the capital for examination. Cai's life story is a typical characterization of these traditions.

The strict Confucian social and political ladder put scholar elite on the top and, compare with them, the uneducated actors and actresses have to stay in a low class-rank not worthy for a dignitary mention, such as similar to that of a prostitute. They were treated despicably as serving people for pleasure only, even though they also inspired truth in life. To perform on stage, either in an imitative way or by impersonating actions, was considered a deceptive practice and seldom associated with virtue. Therefore, the social mobility system severely delayed the progress of theatrical arts in China. A briefing on the insignificance of drama started in court for entertainment might shed some light on the social status of drama in traditional China.

Comedians (優人) as witty characters in farce mark the beginning of Chinese drama. It was said, as early as King Jie (桀) of Xia (夏 ?2205–?1766 BC) and King You (幽王) of Western Zhou (西周 722–481 BC), that there were jesters and dwarfs entertaining the Court.[2] Engaged only in witty gestures and simple dancing steps to music, they mainly cracked jokes or acted ridiculously but were never considered significantly as artists. Some of them did perform to admonish the court in a roundabout way. For example, a jester played the deceased Prime Minster, Sun Shu-au (孫叔敖) in the Chu (楚) court and a dwarf who was skillful in joking also was considered well-versed in offering advice in the Qin (秦) court.[3] This kind of performance went through a monotonous track for many centuries and was treated as nonsensicality in the court of feudal society.

Progressing to the Tang period (618–907 AD), the increasing influence of music from the West territory, Xi Yu (西域), gave new life to the theatrical arts. A few musical plays dealing with real life were presented in the Tang court, such as *Dai Mian* (代面), *Po Tou* (潑頭), *Ta Yao Niang* (踏搖娘). In addition, a popular farce called *San Jun Xi* (參軍戲) was performed with two characters having witty dialogue, a major performer (San Jun參軍), and a clown or assistant character (Cong Gu蒼鶻). This could be the first record of a comedian talk show or the beginning of farce in Chinese history. Although San Jun Xi (參軍戲) as such had not yet developed into a full scale drama with set forms and complicated scripts, it marks a great leap forward in the development of funny characters on the Chinese stage. It was not until the rise of storyteller-based entertainment in the Song Dynasty (宋 960–1279 AD) that broad-scoped and complicated lengthy scripts were presented on stage due to the prosperity of urban centers in China. When drama further matured around the twelfth century, rules and regulations to classify characters were gradually developed.

Therefore, from the beginning of Chinese civilization to the Qing period of late nineteenth century, the theatrical profession was never developed to be recognized as a meaningful trade. Actors and actresses in court did not enjoy a respected role and their acts were not refined. Under the growing prominence of the Confucian sociopolitical system, drama remained as a profession in the lowest spectrum of social class. In fact, men and women could not perform together or live in the same dwelling as a theatrical group until the beginning of the twentieth century. This harsh treatment forced upon them hampered the advancement of classic Chinese drama to become a "performance art" admired for revealing a philosophical interpretation of life among intellectuals as it was in the West.

In Western civilization, drama and other performing arts were developed to have an independent life as entertainment. Dramas and novels were not assessed according to a strict Confucian social and political hierarchy as a low-class achievement not worthy for a dignitary to mention. They were treated as an art for enjoyment while also having the capacity to signify philosophical truths in life. On the contrary, under the dominance of Confucianism, the theatrical arts and novels in China have never been recognized equally as a significant art form similar to painting or poetry. Entertainment was, and still is, considered a service to meet people's pleasure in Chinese society and thus is viewed as an activity with low social status.

This is why, for example, when the delegates who followed the highest Ching Dynasty (1644–1911AD) envoy Lee Hung-zhang (李鴻章) to Europe in the late 1890s reported back to the imperial court of their shocking experience watching how theatrical people mixed socially with royalties and elite officials. Their reports quickly attracted attention in China.

ON WRITING DRAMA

Closely tied to their public careers as officials, the elite gentry's scholars also directed literary trends through their writing, combining aesthetic and moral traditions. Their works were prestigious because their poetry, essays, memos in court, and correspondence between themselves were full of concerns and philosophical thoughts on social issues. Only officially recorded works under their names as influential statesmen were considered refined literature. Witty characters and tragic tales that were written in a lively style for commoners can hardly be found in these scholars' public literary collections. By these standards, for centuries, drama and novel writing, with many shared episodes, were considered "neighborhood gossip" or "small talk" and even the language—mainly vernacular style—was considered quite crude and of little literary merit. This made drama and novels an outlaw of literary works. Formal education would completely exclude this literature even to the turn of the twentieth century. Thus, under the dominance of Confucianism, drama in traditional China had never been recognized as an art form like painting or poetry, nor did it enjoy the same literary prestige as did its Western counterparts.

Dramatists were fully aware of the limitation of their works being sociologically inferior. One cannot expect most of the script writers of Song, Ming and Ching times to seriously take drama writing as a profession. Closely following social development with philosophical metaphors in dramatic writing, as was done in the West during the Renaissance, was not practiced in China. Masters of many great novels and dramas were poor scholars rejected by civil examination. They poured their talents into writing for self-amusement while enduring frustration. However, some of the frustrated officials or civil service literati of no consequence at their time did write dramas and novels of assorted human activities, which proved to be excellent literature of profound quality. To name just a few, Wu Chang-ling (吳昌齡)'s *Dream of Dong Po* (東坡夢) and Li Shou-qing (李壽卿)'s *Lament for the Skeleton* (嘆骷髏), are both great dramas in terms of their entertainment and philosophical value.

The work of dramatists provided more variegated dealings with human and social activities in comparison with that of the Confucian scholars. Some of them must have retained their own popularity and were quite appealing to the masses in their life time and, in some cases, even the members of the royal court. But their profound accomplishments, though fully recognized and treasured today, were only discovered centuries later. In general, this happened more often for novelists than dramatists of the Ming and Qing periods, because novels are more engaging and entreat readers more so than dramatic scripts when singing and actions are absent. But most of the episodes adopted by drama were from novels. Shi Na-an (施耐庵), Luo Guan-zhong (羅貫中), Wu Cheng-en (吳承恩), Wu Jing-zhi (吳敬梓), Cao Xui-qing (曹雪芹) and their works are popularly read and also performed in the theatre. So too is the work of Tang Xian-zu (湯顯祖), Shao Wen-ming (邵文明), Gao Ming (高明), Guan Han-qing (關漢卿), Wang Shi-pu (王實甫), and Yao Mao-liang (姚茂良).

TOPICS AND PRESENTATION OF CHINESE DRAMA

Now familiarized with the aforementioned social and cultural traditions, one can enter the world of Chinese drama with better preparation. If philosophical examination and illustration of social conflict or human nature have not been the focus of Chinese drama, what subject matter has been culturally significant? How do the Chinese present their dramatized life on stage? The traditions have cast the drama and novels from the Yuan to the Ming period into a pre-molded story-telling structure. From a Western point of view, most classical Chinese dramas are a mixture of happy and sad occasions like life itself. The abundance of dramas written during the Yuan and Ming periods mostly fall into the category of the bittersweet tale. Most of them can be termed as stories of suffering with a joyful ending.

Chinese drama and short stories present tales containing "excellent descriptions of society and manners, joy and sorrow, separations and reunions"[4] of a wide range of people in urban centers. The characters in these vernacular stories represented a broad spectrum of social classes, mainly dealing with urban life during a period most typically Chinese (Yuan, Ming and Qing 1279–1912). Tragic events are usually presented at the beginning of a tale to induce courage and bravery, then a happy ending comes in time to cheer the audience. Miserable conditions in life are presented to teach the value of endurance. To overcome difficulties in life seems a task for everybody. For men, life's purpose aimed at nothing but the successful passing of the civil examination and, for women, service and chastity. A character was clearly stage-crafted from the beginning as either virtuous or indecent. Social justice was usually illustrated with an ending rewarding the benevolent and punishing the evil. Codes for moral behavior were clearly laid out and eventual happy endings were expected. Many dramas would promptly end as soon as life's glorious moment was achieved.

This kind of layout not only most efficiently created the blissful and joyful effect of the plot, but also met the purpose of communicating prevailingly positive moral teachings. Values such as courage, dignity, and ethical living were fostered to bring justice for happiness. Famous Yuan dramas *Pei Du Returned the Jade Belt* (裴度還帶) and *Respect Always after Married* (舉案齊眉) are the most directly plotted ones. Ming dramas *The Jade Pin* (荊釵記), *Tale of the Lute* (琵琶記), and *White Rabbit* (白兔記) are a few typical examples of hundreds that are dramas about bearing hardship.

The narrators of Chinese dramas might not use the character to illustrate a philosophical message, plotted accordingly, like in some of the Western drama or novels. But, reading dramatic scripts, the delightfully complicated affairs and portrayal of characters are surprisingly imaginative and movingly compassionate. For instance, Yuan drama *Advising Husband by Killing A Dog* (殺狗勸夫) and the later Ming version, *To Kill the Dog* were cleverly narrated. A virtuous wife saved a drunken husband from moral turpitude by disguising a bloody dead dog as a murdered man to frighten him. She successfully helped her husband redeem his conscience and become a husband who is good to his brother and eventually disassociated from his friends in a local gang. The absurd trick used to reestablish the trust between brothers is a little sarcastic but entertaining. The scheme has hypothetically and psychologically effectuated an unusual tale.

Other than topics rendering a moral message and the usual love stories between literary scholars and their ladies, fictionalized historical events or court cases are the most favored stories among Chinese people. They occupy a large portion of drama in China, especially of the Yuan period. It mostly because the many dramatized ornate stories of the Song period were inherited by Yuan dramatists. The long volume of prompt books by Song story tellers provided numerous episodes for dramatists of later ages, such as *The Tang Tripitaka's Journey Seeking Sutras to the West* (唐三藏西天取經) and *Romance of the Three Kingdoms* (三國演義). In addition, popular tales like *The Loyal National Hero, Yue Fei* (岳飛) (精忠記), *The Political Scheme Using Diao Chan* (貂蟬) in *Lian Huan Jin* (連環記), *Han Xin Begs for Food* (韓信乞食) by Wang Zhong-wen (王仲文), *Wu Hou's Dinner Party* (五侯宴) by Guan Han-qing (關漢卿), *Wu Yuan Plays the Flute* (伍員吹簫) by Li Shuo-qing (李壽卿), and *The Lonely Journey of Guan Yu* (千里獨行) about the hero Guan Yu (關羽) who was captured by Cao Cao (曹操), are the best examples. They are not just straightforwardly narrated tales with a moral message, but unofficial fictional history lessons for illiterate country folks. The heroes or heroines in these tales often win battles by demonstrating courage, dignity, and patriotism to the nation.

As one can see, Chinese drama has dealt mostly with mundane affairs and is scarcely dotted with philosophical satires. Wrongdoings such as killing and lacking filial piety or chastity are expected to be judged at the end of the story. One has to appreciate Chinese dramas as they were produced centuries ago in traditional society. It is in vain for many modern scholars trying to differentiate the huge number of classical Chinese dramas into tragedy (悲劇) or comedy (喜劇), especially based on theoretical definitions of Western drama.

As to the presentation of Chinese Beijing opera, the format on stage is an art belonging to its own style and time that could not be easily renovated to deal with the involution of compound social conditions. With a set format of acting, prescribed music and singing, limited role of cast, the Chinese opera imposed on the performer an extremely difficult training. The players not only had to master the music and lyrics of the whole play but were also required to receive vigorous physical training and personal discipline to be able to perform martial arts and endure the hardship of theatrical life. A repertoire of over a hundred historical events and classical tales already constituted an enormous amount of literature. Opera performers would spend years studying the music and lyrics before they were able to deliver a dramatic piece. By the end of the Ching period, Chinese classic opera had exhausted all the talent and imagination in plot planning and music composing. Hundreds of drama in Beijing opera remained with their original style of performance and plot of the Imperial past, like what classical literature in modern day China. Most of the intellectuals would not devote their talent to create more plays. The performing arts circle as well as the audience in China was ready to receive a new style of theatrical arts.

OUTLOOK ON LIFE

Many Renaissance plays were intended to illustrate an awakening to the worth of humanity beyond the force of a creator. The rise of individualism and self-realization prompted drama to have heroes and heroines stand out with individual characters. They are the offspring of an intellectual revolution which " . . . challenged the meaning attached to existence by the theological leaders of the Middle Age and declared, . . . in favor of interpreting life in purely mundane or human terms."[5] Since China has never been overwhelmingly dominated by a religious power as was Europe in the medieval age, struggle for individual human expression against such a power was not a significant topic in Chinese traditional drama. The exhibition of individual character or inquiry into human nature was not a big literary chapter in the Yuan and Song-Ming periods. Wrestling with philosophical questions on the existence of human race and conflict between social classes were not intended by Chinese dramatists either. This is because, under the "monarchy mandated by Heaven," the civil examination system help break through the class barriers. As discussed before, what was presented in Chinese drama was the essential spirit of moral commitment to kinship living. To ardently observe the norms of ethical behavior among clan and family members is definitely held as a strong basis for human relation. This is most obviously the social background of Ming dramas.

Confucian moral customs were so subtly rooted that they left little space for other schools of thought to provoke arguments. However, though the Taoist outlook on life was vaguely defined and stimulated little energy to counter the influence of the Confucian school, it persisted quite strongly. The cultural forces planted by the Taoist school are quite comparable to those of the Confucian teachings. To reach harmony is one of the cultural goals that the Chinese have deeply conformed to. The Chinese observed and realized a "Natural Way" (Tao) that was forever existing, rejuvenating, and nourishing all things in the universe. Its spirit of embracing everything, including human beings, demonstrates the non-discriminating and loving principle of the Tao. Intellectually, it inspired an individual free spiritedness to rise beyond the entanglement of the mundane human relation web. Religiously, this early philosophical thought. when domesticated with original folk traditions, became the Taoist religion seeking immortality. Consequently, Taoism, at the philosophical or popular level, added a cultural attitude to Confucian moral living—compromise, accepting fate, and agreeing not to be sharp or engage in self-amplification. The utmost happiness of human living was presented as not only diligently seeking wealth and power for family living but achieving harmony with the people around you. Therefore, the Chinese inclined to be humane and humble. They cherished and expected all human affairs to end happily with justice even when great sacrifice had to be called upon. Legends and fairytales almost all ended satisfactorily. Likewise, in theater, the audience did not like to find themselves in tears going home. There were great efforts in the Chinese theatrical world to rewrite and change many tragedies to ended happily in response to popular demand. For example, *Romance of The West Chamber* (西廂記) has at least two versions in Beijing opera, one ending sadly and one happily. Even the great tragedy, *The Injustice Done to Dou E* (竇娥冤), has two endings.

WOMEN IN LOVE AND MARRIAGE

It is necessary to give some thought on the life of women as presented in Chinese drama. Reflecting most realistically the man-centered traditional society, almost all women on stage are symbols of the virtuous codes and are not to be educated so that talent and intellect could be developed. The cultural encompassment has been quite biased to them. The clan centered living founded by the Confucian school prescribed their good fortune with formal marriage (even with a simple ceremony) and service in the family. From Taoism, the attitude of achieving harmony was extended most readily in the lives of traditional Chinese women. For the sake of being well-fitted to family living, women had to be self-forfeiting, constantly compromising, and forgiving. When dramatized stories were presented on stage, married women were always the suffering party. So many dramas entrust women with enduring the hardship of the family while separated from husbands. To win tears from the audience or plot highlights from the drama, harsh circumstances were created particularly for them so that virtues such as loyalty, filial piety, diligent, honesty, and chastity could be revealed.

Nevertheless the worst and most often-presented scenario of many dramas is a virtuous woman's submission or concession to the "happy family reunion (大團圓) settlement" at the end of a drama. Numerous dramas stressed the struggle of a man preparing for the civil examination. All the extra-marital love affairs, separations, and reunions are happenings tied with this purpose of life. With satisfaction, the audience was always entertained with a big reunion settlement in which two women would live "happily ever after" with one husband. The circumstance that contributed to this kind of ending was none other than a separation from home caused by a man's successful achievement. Oftentimes, as soon as a husband successfully passed the civil examination and was appointed to a high position, he most likely either was favored by a prestigious family in the capital to marry its daughter or would fall in love with another woman out of gratitude. The virtuous first wife, no matter how much hardship that she had borne for her husband and his family, seemed most willingly to accept the betrayal of her husband and happily accept his second wife. On quite a few occasions, it was the well-to-do husband and his second wife who rescued the lost and poverty stricken "first wife." The virtuous first wife then consented to the arrangement, joyful to be included again in the family. No anguished feeling on her part was ever mentioned, and, sometimes, the second wife was even praised for her action. *The Tale of the Lute* (琵琶記) exemplifies this straightforwardly. When a hero brought home his so-called second wife after a long-endured separation and hardship, the wife usually accepts the situation and supposedly lives happily ever after. Most amazingly to modern readers, all stories of this kind would end abruptly with no comments added. The simple ending was always presented swiftly and finished satisfactorily in a "matter of fact" manner. It makes the settlement sound so perfectly profound for everybody: the parents, all family members, and the audience at large. Wealth and power reward the man, plus all women (wives) are willing to live with him together. The individual feelings of the two women involved was never a big concern.

To mention just a few, in Yuan drama, *Xiao Xiang Raining Night* (瀟湘夜雨) and *The White Rabbit* (白兔記) are popular dramas with scenarios similar to *The Scholar Zhang Xie* (張協狀元). People shed tears listening to the hardships and sad encounters of the wife. To condemn the heartless behavior of the husbands in betraying their wife was usually executed by demotion of official position. The marriage arrangement of two wives living with one virtuous man seems not quite out of the norm and against custom. No law or judicial authority ever ruled against this kind of "happy ending." The dramatists never intended to bring up a case that would question the merit of the happy ending. How can one not conclude that in addition to the Confucian tradition of testing women's virtues with hardship and encouraging a compromising attitude in life, this kind of "happy family reunion (大團圓) settlement" must be sourced from the Taoist principle of harmony? One has to admit that the large number of classic Chinese dramas with this kind of ending were a reflection of real life in ancient China.

Love is a sacred topic and most beautiful emotion cherished in Western as well as modern Chinese dramas. But in the case of classical Chinese drama, the sweet love of a young couple was not singled out or adoringly described as in modern dramas. Other ethical values are always involved. For example, *Respect Always after Married* (舉案齊眉), a Yuan drama praises the virtue of love and respect between married couples. Most marriages were arranged by family or a matchmaker. The marriage of a couple in love was usually involved with family affairs. Some ended happily after a long struggle in the love affair of a young scholar and the daughter of an affluent family, such as in *Peony Pavilion* (牡丹亭), *Romance of West Chamber* (西廂記), and *To Elope with Xiang Ru* (私奔相如). Whereas the depiction of love affairs between couples of elite family were many, love affairs between prostitutes and young or married man were numerous and elaborately described. Taking the fact that Chinese dramas are incredibly real in mirroring traditional society, we could speculate that a wife played a prescribed role, staying in the household to care for the family and perform daily chores. Social activities would exclude them and take place in the so-called house of entertainers, a combination of a house of prostitution and a modern night club. *Embroidered Robe* (繡襦記), *Ya Xian Saved Yuan He* (亞仙助元和), *Green Mountain* (青山記), and *The Fan of Yao Tao* (夭桃紈扇) are typical examples of dramas that deal with these love affairs.

In addition, with surprise, quite a few plays demonstrate the equally clever and genius qualities of a woman under the great oppression of the male-dominated society of that time. Yuan drama has numerous characters of this nature, such as Guan Han-qing (關漢卿)'s Zhao pian-er (趙盼兒) in *Saved the Unfortunate Lady* (救風塵) and Tang ji-er (譚記兒) in the *Pavilion of Wang Jiang Ting* (望江亭). The extraordinary heroic engagement of Zhao pian-er (趙盼兒) to rescue a sworn sister from being abused made her a brave but somewhat ferocious feminist. Tang ji-er (譚記兒) saved her own marriage with a well-devised plan. Her courage and brightness were admired and the comic effect of the play was brilliantly achieved by the plot. If there were any demonstration of individual daring against injustice, these are good examples. The heroic behavior of the women in these dramas demonstrated humanity among friends and were framed by the core teachings of Confucian ethics, the Five Relations (五倫).[6] Their courage and wisdom helped them endure hardship and achieve success and the happiness of family living.

YUAN DRAMA ACHIEVED AS A LITERARY STYLE

In reviewing the history of Chinese literature, the Yuan dramas are considered more as literature than separately as drama. Unlike its Western counterpart, traditional Chinese drama carried unique features that distinguish it as more valuable as literature than as a play. It was composed of lyrical poetry that constituted the salient part of a play and its most profound feature. Different from the Shakespearean style, the lyrics, as a distinct literary genre, stand out amongst the vernacular dialogue that was sung by the leading roles. From Yuan drama to Ming-Qing Kun drama (崑曲) till today's Beijing opera, only lyrics are accompanied by music in the performance. As the music, acting, and dance of early drama faded away throughout the ages, the original scripts subsisted with lyrical poetry and fragmented dialogues. A huge number of plays dating from the Yuan (1279–1358 AD) to the end of Qing period (1644–1912) are preserved in this manner. Even though they no longer can be staged, the poetry and lyrics remain unshaken for their unique aesthetic literary value. Maybe, originally, the singing and actions on stage diverted people's attention from appreciating the splendor of these lyrics. The literary aspect of drama, however, with the exquisite beauty of the lyrics, became more distinguished in the written scripts and has been recognized as such into the modern era.

For example, the well-known short verse, "Autumn Thought" (秋思), by Ma Zhi-yuan (馬致遠1260?–1334?), is beloved by Chinese. In his lyrics, Ma presented in his a scene of a setting sun with a lone heartbroken traveler:

> Withered vines, old trees, crows at dusk:
> A small bridge, flowing water, a few houses
> An ancient road, a lean horse in the west wind[7]

The many long lyrics in Ma's play *Autumn in Han Palace* (漢宮秋) have lyrics of forty lines sung by the emperor admitting his love and desire after meeting Zhao-Jun (昭君). Zhao Jun, a court lady, stayed with the Han Emperor for a few days before she was sent to marry the Tartar Khan. Helplessly having fallen in love and regretful, the emperor sang in the palace recalling the moment seeing her off: "Slowly, slowly, I lift my cup of jade: If I could but delay this final hour" and "How could I bear to look when last she turned." Her loveliness brushed his heart, when he returned and saw her portrait.[8]

These are just few elegant examples. Besides Ma Zhi-yuan (馬致遠), other leading dramatists, Guan Han-qing (關漢卿), Wang Shi-pu (王實甫), and Bai Pu (白朴) and the hundreds of script writers of the succeeding periods wrote numerous lyrics which elevated the literary aesthetic value of Chinese drama. They left to the Chinese a collection of classical dramas to be treasured and appreciated not just as scripts of plays, but as poetry. Drama, a newly emerged literary work in Yuan time, was able to replace the literary trend of lyric in the Song period because the heritage of Chinese rhymed composition had been carried out by these dramatists. Song rhymed literature as a major trend did not suddenly die out under the rule of the Mongolian empire, but survived in drama, another kind of literary work. The demonstration of literary excellence by these dramatists was particularly significant because their lyrics in the narrative of the drama on stage elevated the status of classical drama as a performing art. Famous works such as *Autumn in Han Palace* (漢宮秋), *The Injustice Done to Dou E* (竇娥冤), *The Firmiana Rain* (梧桐雨), and *The Romance of the West Chamber* (西廂記) have all be designated as representative of classical Chinese drama by encyclopedias in France, the United States, Britain, Japan, and Korea.

Reading the superiorly written lyrics of these dramas, one naturally has the urge to search for their authors and to learn about their educational and literary training. Because of the long- lasting social tradition, writers of novels and drama have never gained a social status equal to those of the elite scholars who wrote poetry and court memos signified by their gentry class. The inferior social status of the Chinese theater and writers of drama has overshadowed the excellent literary quality of their works for a long time. Not only did the authors not enjoy the fame as they should have in their lifetime, but their lyrics of excellent aesthetic quality were also overlooked and buried as if they had been written anonymously. Then, this is why the birth of Yuan drama and an account of its writers in particular deserves our attention. Yuan drama was the first and foremost of the literary productions in China that blossomed under political oppression. The accomplishment of

Yuan dramatists was an illustration of the literati's reaction to severe political persecution. Without an astonishing historical event, Chinese theatre and drama would not have emerged as significant literary entertainment. The vigorous expansion of the Mongol empire during the thirteenth century brought the prosperity of urban life to China. Trade activities with Central Asia and beyond increased enormously. But, the earth-shaking change of the political and social environment caused the loyal Chinese literati to experience the oppression of a foreign conquering power like never before. With the abolishment of the civil examination, Chinese elite intellectuals were at a total loss with no ladder to attain officialdom. Great literary talents were stripped of all their social prestige as they were dispersed to various levels of lower social classes, like prostitutes and beggars. Learned scholars had to step out of their studio and entered the real world of commoners. This oppression directed the talents of many scholars and elite intellectuals of the gentry to write drama entertaining the merchants and Mongols. Unable to participate in public affairs as elite officials, they disposed of their frustration and opinions by creating plots with all kinds of characters who metaphorically indicated their feelings and extricated their misery from oppressive social conditions. Bare vulgarity or folk humor was used to expose the daily happenings of common households. Most of all, they found a channel to cohere their literary profession and demonstrate their literary talent. The shaping of drama with beautiful lyrics inlayed in metrical formats on stage might not be so uniquely structured if literary intellectuals had not participated and articulated their profession.

It was this historical sharp turn that laid the foundation for the flourishing of drama in China. It was also the splendid lyric poetry that made Yuan drama survive as written works and accepted as the representative literary style for Yuan period. Of these great dramatists, Guan Han-qing (關漢卿), Ma Zhi-yuan (馬致遠), and Wang Shi-pu (王實甫) were all literati of great talent, but abandoned their hope for public service. Guan was well-versed in a wide range of knowledge: he was an accomplished poet, calligrapher, and musician. His abundant work struck the heart and soul of the Chinese with fascinating tales for the ages. He impressed people as a dramatist of realism by mirroring the suffering and struggle of the oppressed in the Yuan time. He liked to make use of historical events in his plays. In particular, he had deep sympathy for women, which motivated him to constantly encourage them to rebel against unjust treatment. He voiced their being deprived from the free choice of marriage and condemned the operation of prostitutes. His carefree style and genuine personality was manifested through the characters of his plays. He often designated the female role to reflect his dissatisfaction toward the authority and made them heroines to condemn the corrupted and achieve his will for justice. His *Wang Jiang Ting* (望江亭) and *Xie Tian Xiang* (謝天香) are good examples. He composed forty some plays and over two dozen contained an individual exquisite dramatic lyric piece (散曲) of quality. Because of his prolific talent, he won the title of the King of Chinese drama. Ma and Wang both had a short life of officialdom and became dedicated dramatists. Besides his master piece, *Autumn in Han Palace* (漢宮秋), Ma has at least seven dramatic scripts, 104 short lyrics, and seventeen long lyric compositions that are still on record today. He was famed as the Prince of Short Verse and loftily portrayed himself in his work as one who despised worldly fame and wealth. Wang was especially praised for his elegant and resplendent composition of verse. Inclined to write love stories, Wang wrote his masterpiece, *Romance of West Chamber* (西廂記), which, as the everlasting drama of China, attracted the discussion of international literary scholars.[9] All of this shows that the writing of drama was the accomplishment of a group of literati from the very beginning.

Of the succeeding periods, when Han people regained the sovereign of China, the writers of dramas and novels did not achieve more prestige, but they certainly contributed to the literary composition of drama no less than did their predecessors. Up to the mid-Ming, Kun drama (昆曲) was fashioned with its unique tune of singing. These dramas were still structured by the singing of rhyming passages. Many were written by scholars for self-amusement or as a literary hobby. They were works by literati who either failed the civil examination or became discontent with their official work and refused to get involved in public service. Among the most achieved of these writers were the authors of the Ming time when the development of Kun drama reached its peak. Zhang Feng-yi's (張鳳翼) *Homg Fo Romance* (紅拂記), Liang Chen-yu's (梁辰魚) *Clothes Washing* (浣紗記), Tu Lung's (屠隆) *Tan Flower* (曇花記), Shen Jing's (沈璟) *Green Mountain Screen* (翠屏山), Gu Ta-dian's (顧大典) *Blue Robe* (青衫記), Ye Xian-zhu's (葉憲祖) *Flowery Phoenix* (團花鳳), Tang Xian-zu's (湯顯祖) *Resurrection* (還魂記) or *Peony Pavilion* (牡丹亭) and *Nan Ke Dream* (南柯記). Extending to the Qing period, *Palace of Longevity* (長生殿) by Hong Sheng (洪昇), and *Peach Fan* (桃花扇) by Kong Shang-ren (孔上任) were all popular dramas of excellent literary quality.

DRAMA AND THE NOVEL

The close relationship between drama and the novel in China also testifies to the literary quality of Chinese drama. Classical novels and short stories constantly fed dramas with elaborate plots. Novels with fascinating tales and legends, when dramatized on stage, satisfied the need of the commoners to be entertained. As vernacular tales emerged in the Song (960–1279 AD) and Ming (1368–1644 AD) collection of short stories, they shared with drama the essential features of the original Song oral recitals, which were carried through to the development of Beijing opera. Like twin brothers, many narratives of Ming drama and novels were of the same version, such as *Romance of Three Kingdom*s (說三國), *Autumn in Han Palace* (漢宮秋), and *The Tang Tripitaka's Journey Seeking Sutras to the West* (大唐三藏取經詩話). When dramatized on stage, parts of the dialogues would be transposed to suit the play. For example, *The Romance of West Chamber* (Xi Xiang Ji西廂記) was originally a story written by Yuan Zhen (元稹) of the Tang period. Tong Jie-yuan (董解元), a Song scholar, elaborated it to become a long novel. Then Wang Shi-pu (王實甫) put it on stage as drama.

Traditionally, the Chinese considered the dramatists Guan Han-qing (關漢卿) and Wang Shi-pu (王實甫) together with novelists such as Shi Na-an (施耐庵) and Wu Cheng-en (吳承恩) as accomplished writers in literature. In fact, early translations of Western drama, such as Shakespeare's *Henry the Fifth* and *The Merchant of Venice* and Henrik Ibsen's *Hedda Gabler* were all read and treated as literature in China. Consequently, besides investigating the Western theory of drama, the modern literary reformers, Zhu Guang-qian (朱光潛) and Xiong Fo-xi (熊佛西), should have an in-depth understanding of the Chinese drama from a literary point of view.[10] Upon learning a new branch of foreign literary work and amazed by the Western world of drama, their insight on literary aspects of Chinese drama will help them to be objective.

MUSIC AND LYRIC IN DRAMA

Originating from early folk lyrics, Tang poetry and Song lyrics and verses principally all have a rhyming and tonal structure which is exhibited together with their accompanying musical pattern. The musical structure, developed during and after Song period accompanied the formation of Yuan and Southern drama (南曲), is the major element of Chinese drama. The strict four acts and an add-on interpretation part (楔子), if needed, in Yuan drama was shaped reciprocally by the music elaborately developed then. The composition of each act mainly depended on how the individual lyrics were arranged together according to harmony of music. Not only are the rules and regulations of tone and rhythm strictly laid out for wording, but the number of lyrics grouped in each act is also limited. Conforming to the tone and rhythm of the lyrics, a dramatist then can display his rhetorical talent to fill each metrical form with a string of genuine terms. The metrical forms of some lyrics in drama may have to be developed to different length from that of Tang and Song poetry. In answering the arrival of new tones with the empire's expansion of territory, drama in Yuan and other dynasties had to be elaborately composed by embracing new metrical format. Without sensitivity in the music, a dramatist will fail the test of carrying out the heritage of rhyming literature.

In view of the dual quality of Chinese theatrical art, Chinese drama was produced under bilateral demands, entertaining the general public and satisfying the ego of the literati for aesthetic expression. Thus, the singing of the lyrics that were written to signify or summarize the choicest part of the play became the quintessential aspect of the show. The musical life of the many lyrics sprung into the spotlight when featured in drama. Stage backdrop, dialogues, and actions were all simplified to make the singing part more outstanding as the center of attention. Singing was limited to one or two major roles, putting the actions and performers at ease. This kind of musical performance is actually quite similar to that of the modern musical in the West, such as *The Phantom of Opera* or *West Side Story*, except the lyrics in Chinese drama are more structured with a tonal format than are the freestyle verses of Western songs. Anyhow, the tradition that Chinese audiences come to the theatre to "listen" to the drama (聽戲) instead of "watch" the show (看戲) further confirms the literary development of Chinese drama.

Even though Chinese drama as a whole did not go through a philosophical orientation, the aesthetic literary value remains most profound. There is an inseparable and essential literary value in the Chinese dramas and novels of the Yuan to Ming periods. Rhyming literature is shared as a major portion of Chinese literature. When the lyrics of the Song period gradually died out, Yuan drama formally inherited and elaborated it to fit to the new musical tones as the salient part of a play. It was because of the literary value of these lyrics that drama was accepted as a representative literary style of the Yuan period in Chinese history. Although the strict Confucian elite Chinese society did not grant even the least social status to the profession, "tragedy (悲劇)" and "comedy (喜劇)" lured great talents and left an enormous amount of literary works for us to read.[11] They provide an incredible amount of information worth examining to gain an understanding of Chinese social life. The numerous scholars who were rejected candidates in civil examinations poured their talents into producing profound dramas and had to wait until centuries later to be appreciated as great writers.

CONCLUSION

One requires not only a sense of how various dramas should be seen and heard, but also an understanding of the social and cultural conditions that produced these dramas to appreciate them beyond one's native intellectual realm. Both Chinese and Western dramas were developed within the web of their respective civilizations. They recapitulate and present the essence of their traditions. Long ignorant of each other's existence, the East and West created a cultural environment for their drama styles and retained their original character for a long time.

NOTES

1. Four Ethical Principles (四維): Propriety, Justice, Honesty, Shame of not being virtuous (禮義廉恥). Eight Cardinal Virtues (八德): Loyalty, Filial-piety, Benevolence, Love, Trustworthiness, Righteousness, Harmony, and Peace (忠孝仁愛信義和平).

2. Liu Xiang (77 BC–6 AD) of the Han Dynasty (206 BC–220 AD), recorded in the *Biography of Ancient Women of Virtue* the story of the dissolute King Jie and his beloved concubine: "He gathered jesters, dwarfs, and people of prostitute society who could do strange tricks around him and play romantic but bad taste music." In the chapter, "Zeng Yu" of the book *Guo Yu*, it is written that "Shi Bo talked to Zeng Huan Gong about King You of Zhou. Dwarfs and flatterers are always accompanying him in the court. The *Book of History* said about these people: 'They are all Jesters to fawning people and make them laugh'" 劉向，古烈女傳，孽嬖傳載：桀。。。收倡優侏儒狎徒能為奇偉戲者，聚之于旁。造爛漫之樂。國語，鄭語，史伯對鄭桓公說周幽王．侏儒，戚施實御在側。書昭曰：侏儒，戚施，皆優笑之人。

3. Shi ji, *Biographies of the Witty*, Taiwan Commercial Press .史記，滑稽列傳，台灣商務印書館

4. Lu, Hsun (l959), *A Brief History of Chinese Fiction*. Hyperion Press, Inc., West Point, Connecticut, p. 257.

5. Schevill, Ferdinand, *The Society of the Italian Renaissance*, The Civilization of the Renaissance, Frederick Ungar Publishing Co., New York. P. 60.

6. 五倫， Five Relationships of Kinship Living. Superior (emperor) and Subjects, Father and Son, Husband and Wife, Brothers and Friends.

7. Liu, Wu-chi and Lo, Irving Yucheng, *Sunflower Splendor, Three thousand years of Chinese Poetry*, Anchor Press/Doubleday, p. 420.

8. Birch, Cyril, ed. *Anthology of Chinese Literature, From early times to the Fourteenth century*. Grove Press, Inc. New York, 1965. P. 440–441.

9. Wang, Hong. (王洪) Ed. *A Complete Collection of Yuan Drama* (元曲百科大全). Xue Wan Publish Company (學苑出版社), 1991 北京..

10. Yuan, Guo Xin (袁國興), *The Birth and growth of Chinese Stage Play* (中國話劇的孕育與生成), Wen Jing Publish Company (文津出版社印行). 1993. Chinese Drama Publish Company (中国戏剧出版社) 2000, Taiwan.

11. As will be explained later, "tragedy" and comedy" are here in quotation marks as drama in Chinese should really be categorized by "tragedy literature (悲劇文)學" or "comic literature (喜劇文學)" because it encompasses a broader domain that includes features such as poetry and lyric.

Part II

On Drama, East and West

Chapter Three

The Coming of Western Drama

This chapter gives a briefing on the entering of Western stage drama to China and in what way it was received by Chinese intellectuals in the initial stage. The development of the modern stage play (話劇) in China went through a process where many factors contributed to the way in which the traditional environment perceived the new style. Comparative studies on the characters of theatre and drama of the East and West have been carried out productively. But the social environments that caused the fast development of new drama have not been examined thoroughly. It is interesting to review the entrance of Western stage drama into China and the initial reception it received from Chinese intellectuals.

BACKGROUND: INTELLECTUAL REFORM AND CHINESE LITERATURE

By the mid-1800s, China had been too long in isolation and too deeply corrupted to avoid domestic depression. Unfortunately for China, it was also a time when Western colonial powers, energized by advanced science and technology, stepped up their forays into Asia. The incessant wars against colonial invaders from the West and the resultant unrest weakened the old Chinese empire. China had virtually no chance of asserting her dignity by defending her territory or remaining on an equal footing with these foreigners. And, of course, the social conditions in China then furnished Westerners with hardly any incentives to properly understand the significance of China's cultural traditions or the strength of China's nationalism. For China, the realization of being defeated and humiliated by technically vigorous Western civilizations was a shocking and bitter lesson. To awake from her downfall and face the technically advanced West was a rough uphill road; China had to fight it out or perish.

It was during this desperate state of affairs that China took to social reforms and tried to shake off its many decadent social traditions by adopting new traits. In response to increasing pressure to catch up with industrialized nations, officials and intellectuals of the late Qing Dynasty (1644–1911 AD) first insisted on a policy of adopting Western scientific knowledge and technology while preserving the Chinese sociopolitical system. This meant that monarchical authority held onto traditional philosophical thoughts and related conventions as the basis for administering the country and applied Western science and technology as tool to modernize the country (中學為體, 西學為用). But the lack of sincerity on the part of the imperial court for reform plus the domestic fighting among factions of the monarchy disappointed the reformers. At the same time, the tidal wave of colonialism brought more intrusions, such as the opium trade and war with the British (1839–1842). The Chinese started to become aware of the fact that China needed not just the West's technology, but the fundamental spirit behind its scientific knowledge as well. They were eventually convinced that the revitalization of China required broadening the arena of renovation to include the social and political systems. In order to do so, extensive study and understanding of the history and culture of the Western nations had to be promoted.

However, before the corrupt and obstinate Qing Dynasty Court could realize any kind of social reform, the drive for a new sociopolitical system modeled after the West intensified and was led forward by a group of revolutionaries. Disillusioned with their confrontations with bureaucratic corruption, groups of intellectuals joined the revolutionary forces lead by Sun Yi-xian (孫逸仙) and established the Republic of China in 1911. The establishment of a democratic republican state in China hastily took place and conclusively ended the days of imperial rule in China. But before a viable constitution for the Republic of China could be thoroughly implemented, China was hit in quick succession by turmoil among Chinese warlords and political factions, as well as incursions from Japan. It would have been a miracle if any of world's secular government could have dealt with the complicated situations that prevailed at the turn of the twentieth century and thereafter in China. The change in China's deplorable fate had to be deferred until as late as the beginning of the 1980s.

However, the 1911 revolution's success lifted the spirits of the Chinese people who were looking forward to the coming of a new age. Realizing the overwhelming power of advanced science and technology and tremendous influence in the life of Chinese people by the West, these Chinese intellectuals voluntarily initiated reform and paved the way to modernization. They were loyally committed to saving China from exploitation by profit-seeking foreign forces, but were at the same time overwhelmingly impressed with the advances in science and technology, and prosperity in the West. Highlighted by their reform during the May Fourth Movement of 1919, writers, poets, scholars of social science and philosophy, and educators at once joined other reformers and took the lead and occupied the center stage in the reform movement. The ultimate purpose of almost all Chinese intellectuals was to seek an understanding of the essential force behind the advances of Western society, including Western sociopolitical systems, cultural values, literature, and philosophical thought. To obtain opportunities for going abroad and to return with new knowledge was everybody's dream at that time. Many came back with only a brief exposure to Western society or a short term of study, but they ardently recounted anything that had caught their eyes.

It was during their study abroad experience that the intellectual thought and philosophical foundation of Western civilization embedded in literature and drama were brought back to China. Reform-minded writers and educators formed an earnest social circle and the public followed with great interest the literary works they wrote to interpret the new knowledge from abroad. This information pounded into the minds of liberal art students like ocean waves on dried sand beaches. Their commitment to make change was unquestionable, but the social and political environment heightened the complexity of getting Western cultures properly accepted, both in terms of counteraction and absorption. They were in those days by far the most influential force on the sociopolitical scene. Of all the new forms of knowledge, Western music, arts, literature and drama were the quickest to catch the attention of the public through the news media. By way of the new vernacular literary style, stage plays flourished and fascinated the minds of Chinese people just as cinema does in today's society.

THE EARLY STUDY OF WESTERN STAGE DRAMA AND ROOTS IN EUROPE

Western stage plays captured the eyes of early reformers when Lee Hongzhang (李鴻章)[1] went to Europe in the late 1890s and was enormously impressed by the elaborate stage decorations powered by electricity there. The Chinese official was surprised to the fact that the performing arts of Europe were an important feature of modern Western civilization, not only respected as a creative art but also as possessing high literary value. According to the diary of Zeng Ji-ze (曾紀澤) (1882), the Chinese ambassador to France, England, and Russia, after the treaty of Frankfurt that ended of Franco-Prussian War in 1871, France recovered its national prestige and strength by building a huge theatre and museum to boost its national pride. Articles and other reports written on the reconstruction of France from overseas drew the attention of the Chinese to the social and patriotic function of the theatre in the West.² Also, the observation by students abroad of the social prestige and popularity of the actors and actresses as well as the theatrical activities in Europe totally overwhelmed the Chinese at home. Respect for novels and drama and their independent life in Western civilizations was most inspiring to the Chinese at that time. Delighted by the philosophically structured plots, ideas, and spirit of Western drama and novels, a small group of Chinese students in Europe started to study Western Drama seriously.

ATTENTION FROM LITERARY SCHOLARS AT HOME

The rise of stage drama was partially stimulated by the Chinese "modernization and rejuvenation" social movement during the 1910s and 1920's. It was a time when the old system was diminished and imported new ones not yet digested. The changes in society had been submitted to the opinions of intellectuals and social phenomena closely monitored in their works. For example, as early as 1903, the social function of drama caught the attention of such intellectuals as Kang You-wei (康有為), Liang Qi-chao (梁起超), Yan Fu (嚴復), Cai Yuan-pei (蔡元培), and Tan Si-tong (譚嗣同). These highly enthusiastic early reformers paid more attention to the effects of Western literary works on sociopolitical change than on the literary values of these works. They promoted the idea that awakening the Chinese people's sense of mobilizing China for progress required much greater reliance on novels and drama. Science and technology were not enough. For example, Liang Qi-chao wrote many plays directly aiming at current social problems. In his *Dream of Destruction* (劫灰夢), he compared the social condition of China to Louis XIV's France and how a dramatist's work could lead his fellow countrymen back to the right consciousness. Chen Du-xiu (陳獨秀) returned from Japan and wrote about the importance of adopting Western drama.³

Therefore, the study of Western drama and plays was intricately tangled up with Chinese intellectuals' attention to social reform. In fact, from the very beginning, these sociopolitical leaders focused more on the social function of drama than on the art of drama itself. This kind of social responsibility with insightful influence entrusted to the performing arts did not happen among elite scholars and politicians in the West.

THE SPARKS OF WESTERN "NEW STAGE DRAMA" ALONG THE COASTING CITIES

Western stage drama entered China through two routes: Shanghai (上海) in the South and Tianjing (天津) in the North. The port city of Shanghai (上海) saw the arrival of an increasing number of Europeans after the late 1890s. Their performing arts activities were mostly confined to small overseas European communities and attracted little attention from the local Chinese. A Christmas program by students of Shanghai's Fan Wang Du (梵王渡) at Christian St. Johns School in the winter of 1898 was the first recorded activity. French Catholic schools, called the "Xu Hui Gong Xue (徐匯公學)," also put on short plays by their students. At the same time, a theater called Lan Xin Play House (蘭心戲院) held regular public performances of short Western dramatic plays three or four times a year. These events marked the earliest activities of "Western Drama" in China and were mostly for the European community.[4]

THE SPRING WILLOW CLUB (春柳社) AND NAN KAI CLUB (南社)

In the early days of the nineteenth century, financial difficulty had prevented many intellectuals from traveling directly to Europe and North American to seek knowledge of Western traditions. Quite a few young Chinese people had to fulfill their quest in Japan through the medium of Japanese-filtered Western culture. It was not until the organization of the Spring Willow Club (春柳社) in Japan[5] by a group of overseas Chinese students in 1910 that the Chinese started to learn about Western stage plays. Western drama had been enthusiastically received in Japan and attracted the interest of overseas Chinese students, such as Zeng Xiao-gu (曾孝谷) and Lu Jing-ruo (陸鏡若). Inspired by the popularity of the Westernized Japanese theater, a group of Chinese students, Wang Zhong-sheng (王鐘聲), Zheng Zheng-qiu (鄭正秋),[6] and Li Shu-tong (李叔同) started the Spring Willow Club (春柳社) with a début performance of the *La Dame Aux Camelias* (茶花女) and *Uncle Tom's Cabin* (黑奴籲天錄) in 1907. Their successful performances were widely publicized back home. The prestigious social status of these students from elite families helped to pave a smooth entrance for stage plays into China. Upon their return to China, Western stage drama was brought back to Shanghai (上海) and gradually acquired an audience among the Chinese public. During its germinal period until 1918, the Spring Willow Club (春柳社) and its followers introduced Western drama to China mainly by way of Japanese sources.

Almost at the same time, Nankai University (南開大學) in the northern port city of Tianjing (天津), started its drama club under the leadership of its founding scholar, Zhang Bo-ling (張伯苓). Zhang went to Europe and America opening up a channel to bring in new Western style drama directly from the West in 1908. He and his brother, Zhang Peng-chun (張彭春) who studied Western drama in the United States (1910–1916), vigorously promoted stage play activities on the Nankai University campus. The Zhang brothers even wrote their own plays, such as *Knowledge Failed in Reality World* (用

非所學) and *Awakening* (醒), and in this way have led the development of modern stage plays in the North since 1916.[7]

As both groups successfully accomplished the initial stage of introducing Western stage drama into China, they also nourished the growth of Chinese stage drama. Without the restrictions of using foreign languages to perform the Western stage play, the modern Chinese stage drama was also freed from all the restrictions of Beijing opera with naturalistic acting and delivery. Riding the tide of the vernacular language movement, actors could convey a dramatic tale with expressions from everyday spoken language. As the social movement in China demanded that the stage drama to function more and more as a voice for such issues as seeking freedom from the family, arranged marriages, or vowing for a democratic political system, the traditional Beijing opera drama was handicapped in addressing current social events. The new stage dramas came in time to effectively present complicated plots without having to capture the audience's imagination with conventional acting or stage settings.

The clubs' initial sparks were smothered in the dust of China's trouble-stricken society, but their plays' dramatic format was readily accepted by the Chinese. The clubs' founding members had never given up their pursuit of drama transmitted from the West, even though it was the foreign roots that made them fall short to be considered as totally "Chinese" by the majority of Chinese people.

PROGRESSIVE SOCIETY (進化團)

It is comprehensible that soon after the 1911 revolution and May Fourth Movement, the new stage drama caught the tide of political and social reform, granted to itself a purpose, and joined the mainstream of each social movement as a powerful example of public media. During the height of the 1911 revolution led by Sun Yat-sen (孫逸先) against the Imperial Qing Court, a politically enthusiastic drama group called Progressive Society (進化團) emerged as a leading performer of the newly adopted stage drama. Espousing China's political and social reforms, it fully undertook the duty as a vanguard for the revolutionary cause. With the society's spirit, its new stage plays ripened to answer soaring angry emotions. These plays were presented in modern dialogue by means of the Western stage play format of usually three or four acts. As early as 1910s, in Nanjing, the organizer of the society, Ren Tian-zhi (任天知) and his friend produced *Sick Man in East Asia* (東亞病夫)[8] and *Bloody Rain Coat* (血蓑衣), which was based on the Japanese play *Bloody Tears* (血之淚).

The plots and presentations of the plays did not strictly follow the formats or newly introduced patterns of Western drama. Instead, political lectures or messages were added, sometimes executed in traditional Chinese dramatic style. These additions helped express the dissatisfaction of the Chinese people toward the corrupt and incompetent Qing dynasty court and exposed the backwardness of many social customs. Energized by the feverish revolutionary spirit, this new drama style became enormously popular and was widely accepted by Chinese audiences. This expansion illustrates precisely the development pattern of a foreign literary style which was gradually perceived and adopted by a culture that already possessed its own rich literary heritage. They adopted the presentation format of the Western stage play and made use of drama to serve the promotion of government policy. No emphasis was placed on developing the aesthetic aspect of performing arts.

FAMILY SOAP-OPERA (家庭戲) AND MODERN STAGE PLAYS (文明戲)

At the same time, the final success of the 1911 revolution set a new political government for the Chinese people, but the new administration suffered from many political hindrances. The modern Chinese theatrical circle was moderately active and the newly established stage dramas were left bewildered about the direction of its social functions. Despite the many setbacks during China's revolutionary aftermath, a brief period of respite of ten years after 1911 gave rise to the so-called "Family Soap-Opera (家庭戲)," or romantic drama. Family Soap-Operas are a number of so-called melodramas by Chinese writers produced with some mixed features of classic Chinese opera and delivered in a modern style setting and with modern clothing (文明戲). Promoted by the New People's Society (新民社) in 1913, these melodramas consisted of romantic and sentimental plays reflecting traditional life in a changing society. Different from the plays produced by both the political minded Progressive Society (進化團) and the Western-flavored Spring Willow Club (春柳社), these melodramas won the support of common households during a short time of rest and prosperity in early Republican China. Tired of being lectured with sociopolitical slogans, the public was entertained and comforted with plays that did not touch upon ongoing social problems. These plays caught the sentiment of the Chinese as stories of common people in their everyday living were staged and represented recurrent Chinese traditions. They reached a broad audience from middle class households to small merchants, cleaning ladies, and women of leisure. They appeared on the Chinese stage with a modern setting, but with costumes and dialogue that were of a mixed style bearing some features of classic Chinese opera. These were truly a combination of the styles of East and West. Oftentimes, they were staged with traditional opera features but eliminated the singing portion, such as in the popular plays, *Mother* (母), *Sisters* (姊妹) and

Yan Zhi Jing (燕支井). In succeeding years, these melodramas were referred as Modern Stage Plays (文明戲). Soon, however, these plays became the targets of critical comments during the tidal wave of the May Fourth Movement and were accused of ignoring the national crisis and relishing materialist enjoyment.[9] Criticized for lacking social and national consciousness, they soon reached their decline. In these early years, the three styles of drama propounded by Spring Willow (春柳社), the Progressive Society (進化團), and the family theatre (文明戲) arose one after another in China's world of performing arts, encapsulating the complexities of Chinese society during that era.

THE GROWTH AND DECLINE OF STAGE DRAMA: LITERARY TRENDS OF EAST AND WEST

As guardians of Chinese tradition and entrusted with serving as China's conscience, the intellectual leading scholars of the 1920s and 1930s had in their minds a mission to modernize the mentality of the Chinese people. They were from educated elite families and the selected few who went to the West for education. Following the rallying cry for a new political and social system modeled after the West, the May Fourth Movement of 1919 was impassioned by a broad study of Western social and political systems, cultural values, and philosophical thought. Committed to this mission, May Fourth scholars included the promotion of modern stage plays as part of their intellectual and social movement. As a result, for a period of time form he 1920s to the 1930s, the Chinese educational circle took notice of a great effort to introduce Western literature.

The Introduction of Western Literature

It has been the case with both Eastern and Western traditions that dramas and novels nurtured each other by sharing narratives. The stage drama in China was also cultivated by the coming of Western literature. Since Western literary styles had long been unfamiliar to the Chinese due to the long mutual isolation of the East and West, a large number of novels and drama by Western authors were translated and introduced to Chinese readers in the 1920s and 1930s. Mention only a few, works by Oscar Wilde, Victor Hugo, Friedrich Schiller, and William Shakespeare were popular from the beginning. Henrik Ibsen, Alexandre Dumas, Molière, Emile Zola, Anton Chekhov, Leo Tolstoy, Fyodor Dostoevsky, Johann Wolfgang Von Goethe, and many others from India and Japan. All in all, some 200 plays from twenty some countries were translated by scholars. Along with novels and short fiction, eighty-one plays by forty-six foreign playwrights were translated and some 115 plays were published by leading publishers, such as Commercial and

Chinese publishers between 1919 to 1924.[10] Tian Han (田漢), an early leading dramatist who was captured by the literary trend of Romanticism, translated altogether nineteen famous plays. These included *La Dame aux Camellias*, plays by Shakespeare (*The Merchant of Venice*, *Hamlet*, and *Romeo and Juliet*), *Carmen*, and quite a few Japanese plays.

There were also a group of Chinese dramatists who led some exciting discussions on the theory of drama. Romanticism's trend of thought had a strong foothold in the Chinese literary circle. Lu Xun (魯迅), Mao Dun (矛盾), and Guo Mo-ruo (郭沫若) had all pioneered to introduce and translate literature by Romantic writers in the 1920s, such as Lu Xun (魯迅)'s *Wen hau pian zhi lun* (文化偏至論) and Guo Mo-ruo (郭沫若)'s translation of works by Schiller and Goethe. Some of them caught the critical spirit of Romanticism and expressed vigorous opposition to the sovereign state system carried throughout imperial China. Some were simply moved by the many poems and novels and wanted their fellow Chinese to appreciate the beauty of Romantic works.[11]

Leading journals also launched discussions on Western literature and drama. And so, supported by its Western literary origins, the new stage drama was, from its beginnings, welcomed by the educated Chinese as having an elite social status.

Performance and Production

The spirit for producing plays on stage was almost as feverish as the introduction of Western literature. There were as many as 400 plays produced in ten years from 1919–1929.[12] In this process, the production went through a journey of transition, gradually shifting from performing Western dramas in the beginning to life and social issues in China. Expression on stage, the script started from free speech to gradually confirmed literary values.

The first stage productions, starting with the establishment of the Spring Willow Club (春柳社) in 1907, were plays that had been performed in Japan by club members and that were later put on stage back in China. Though the format of plays and stage setting were still in a formative time, dramatists and playwrights were still eager to foster the development of adapted Western plays. During the shocking time of 1911, a steady stream of new drama productions spread all over China. Sardou's *La Tosca* (熱血) was the most successful one and aroused spirit for the 1911 revolution. Shanghai was the center in the south and most active in drama performances. There were twelve performance troops with incredibly modernized stage design. Canton further in the south was fascinated by Chen Shao-bai's (陳少白) *Zhen Tian Sheng Ju Tuan* (振天聲劇團), which carried performances in Hong Kong and cities of Southeast Asia. In the North, there were a dozen new plays performed in Beijing, Tianjing, and Manchuria directed by Liu Yi-zhou (劉藝舟).

Some of the activities were part of the Progressive Society (進化團). For the triumphant of the revolution, *Gold and Blood* (黃金赤血) and *Long Live the Republic* (共和萬歲) were popular in Shanghai. Ou Yang Yu-qian (歐陽于倩), Ren Tian-zhi (任天知), Cha Tian-ying (查天影), and Xia Yue-shan (夏月珊) were all the famous actors and actresses who helped to keep the growth of new dramas lively.[13] However, due to the intense social turmoil in China, these highly westernized stage plays that enjoyed popularity among the young people failed to blossom fully at times. They were intermittently flourishing whenever China got a few years of peace and prosperity.

Comparable to the translated foreign plays and the overwhelmingly evolutionary victory plays, there were also beloved Chinese melodramas produced, such as the early productions of *Homeland* (故鄉), *Youth* (青年), and *Trouble at Home* (家庭恩怨記). The production of a two-act stage play, *River Wu* (烏江) by club member Wu Wo-zhun (吳我尊) in 1919 successfully transformed the historical tale of *Goodbye My Love by Ba Lord* (霸王別姬)[14] and adopted traditional Chinese music as the background.

The second period of maturity and prosperity of the dramatic arts was driven by another wave of political movement, The May Fourth Movement. The disappointment on the part of China over the Shan Dong (山東) resolution of the Versailles Peace Conference in 1919 and the insult felt by the Chinese people certainly incited enormous anti-foreign emotion. As the participation of Chinese intellectuals in this social movement erupted in a strong feeling of nationalism, stage drama came in time to carry their mission. A thoughtful mind cannot escape seeing the reality, the culture, history, and life of one's own country and that of others. The exploration of all kinds of philosophical insights on human activity from outside China brought by novels and drama attracted the Chinese enormously. Inspired by the literary trends of thought of Realism and the social status of drama and novels from the West, these writers and scholars sincerely believed that to promote the introduction of Western literature and further the development of a new Chinese stage drama was a worthy mission. Many stage plays helped denounce foreign incursion on the one hand and, on the other, shook the Chinese people's faith and conviction in the viability of their long-standing traditional cultural values. It was this patriotic focus by May Fourth intellectuals and their participation in new dramas that kept stage plays fast growing. If only some theater-loving people had been pushing the production of the new dramas, they might have rolled out the development much slower. Besides Tian Han (田漢), Hong Shen (洪深), and Chen Da-bei (陳大悲), many writers joined the force. Under their collective effort, subject matter was enriched, literary values polished, and style of expression improved, a result of scholarly attainment and artistic sensitivity. They combatted for setting up rules for performance, such as strictly following the script and the sole authority of the director.

Like its roots in foreign lands, the stage play continued with some dramas from the West, but soon took off by presenting the affairs of local society, such as in the most popular play by Hu Shi (胡適), *Marriage* (終身大事), which was based on Ibsen's *A Doll's House*. Bernard Shaw's *Mrs. Warren's Profession* was performed in Shanghai in October of 1920, although it was not well received. The promotion of dramas mostly depended on playwrights returned from abroad. Dramatist Chen Da-bei (陳大悲) helped organize the Ai Mei Club (愛美劇), whose name was transliterated from the English word "amateur." It was a movement that helped initiate casual informal shows among interested groups and then developed professional troupes. There were all together fourteen plays performed every weekend by students in 1923, including Chen's famous plays *The Hero and Beauty* (英雄與美人) and *Lady You Lan* (幽蘭夫人) and Pu Bo-ying's (蒲伯英) *Filial Piety of the Rich* (闊人的孝道). Hong Shen (洪深), a graduate of Harvard, returned to China and dedicated himself to the production of stage plays in Shanghai. His 1924 production, *The Fan of the Fair Lady* (少奶奶的扇子), was an adaptation of Wilde's *Lady Windermere's Fan*. It attracted wide admiration. His transfiguration of the play with character, expression, and circumstances totally fit local taste and the realistic setting of the stage won the cheers of the audience. Shanghai People's Drama Club constantly carried out performances because of Hong's effort. What is most striking about Chen and his dramatist friends' effort was that within a few years, theatrical art institutes and drama classes were established, plus theater troupes were found in big cities all over China. Prominent scholars Liang Qi-chao (梁啓超), Lu Xun (魯迅), Zhou Zuo-ren (周作人), Xu Ban-mei (徐半梅), and Sun Fu-yuan (孫伏園) were all involved. The new drama sentiment was so pervasive that when American-educated dramatists Yu Shang-yuan (余上沅) and Zhao Tai-mou (趙太侔) returned to China, they caught the heat of the wave and founded the Beijing National Theatrical Art Institute. Its 1926 production of *The Night Tiger was Caught* (獲虎之夜) by Tian Han (田漢) and *Oppress* (壓迫) and *A Bee* (一只蜜蜂) by Ding Xi-lin (丁西林) overwhelmingly captured the mind of populace. Thereafter, the development of stage plays by the effort of these dramatists became an integral "function" of the performing arts in China.

The tidal wave of Realism led by Henrik Ibsen and Anton Chekhov in Europe hit China too. The social consciousness of writers and dramatists stoked heat for more realism in plays. Given the name of the Father of Modern Drama in Europe, Ibsen's realistic approach, inquiring into the condition of life and people's morality, responded precisely to the searching spirit of China in the early twentieth century. Ou Yang Yu-qian (歐陽予倩), Chen Da-bei (陳大悲), Tian Han (田漢), Guo Mo-ruo (郭沫若), and Hong

Shen (洪深) were all followers of the realistic school. This school of thought held that plays should: 1) Realistically coincide with the contemporary lifestyle and social trends, 2) Reflect the thought and purpose of people on social reform, and 3) mobilize social change through fiction and dramatized performance. *A Doll's House* and *When the Dead Awaken* were staged in 1914 and articles about Ibsen's plays were published. Even Björnstjerne Björnson was also made known among Chinese dramatists through the promotion of Mao Dun (矛盾).[15]

Therefore, one would expect that Chinese stage plays written by these intellectuals could never be just sketching a tale with no feeling of the complex, confused, and frustrated mood of people in that era. They pitilessly and realistically revealed the dark side of human life, just as Ibsen, who had certain influence in the spirit of the Chinese literary circle, did in his dramas. The vow to change the family structure and political system all became topics for Chinese dramatists. For example, the great novelist, Ba Jin (巴金) gave the literary circle a thunder-like surprise by publishing his masterpieces, *Family* (家), Spring (春), and Autumn (秋), for which stage plays were scripted and dominated the performance arts. With a realist approach, his sharp pen produced many varieties of episodes from rebellion against parents' arranging of marriages to critiques of large family dwellings. His words vowing for individual liberalization were a torch aiming at the abolition of a totalitarian sociopolitical system and decisively addressed social problems of the day. Cao Yu's (曹禺) *Sun Rise* (日出), *Thunderstorm* (雷雨), and *Under the Roof in Shanghai* (上海屋簷下) were sensationally received. With this direction, Chinese stage dramas settled on realistic acting and stage backdrops. They directly depicted current social events without adding analysis. They expressed Chinese emotion and cast opinion on Chinese social reform. The sharp criticism reflected in the script on corruption and other social problems was vividly presented. Many articles were published in this respect in early magazines and journals.[16] In reaction to the movement, a leading college campus in Beijing initiated stage shows to give a united voice to their concern. The new style of drama attracted enormous talent among the young intellectuals and actively spread in college campuses. Contrary to their attitude toward traditional Chinese drama, progressive and prominent families did not prohibit their children from participating in it. College campuses hosted many stage plays with the help of Chen Da-bei (陳大悲). As a result, vigorous plays erupted with anti-authority emotions on college campuses after the end of WWII when social unrest rose again in China.

Fostered by this effort, Chinese newspapers and magazines had also kept pace with literary publications in Europe since the late 1890s. The different schools of Western literature, such as of Late Romanticism and Realism, were introduced by the most influential journal during the May Fourth Movement, *The New Youth* (新青年). In the June issue of 1918, a special section was devoted to a discussion of Ibsen, introducing readers to three of his dramas, *A Doll's House*, *An Enemy of the People*, and *Little Eyolf*. Recommended by Hu Shi (胡適), October's special issue introduced fifty-eight authors from thirteen European countries translated by dramatist Song Chunfang (宋春舫). The Symbolism, Mysticism, and Dilettantism of the Late Romantic schools and their works were discussed and published in journals such as *Novel Monthly* (小說月報), *New Wave* (新潮) and *Eastern Magazine* (東方雜誌). Most of the progressive writers, such as Lu Xun (魯迅), Tian Han (田漢), Guo Mo-ruo (郭沫若), Xu Zhi-mo (徐志摩), Hong Shen (洪深), and Mao Dun (矛盾), were all participants in the discussion. Influential authors such as Hu Shi (胡適), Chen Du-xiu (陳獨秀), and Liu Ya-zi (柳亞子) ere constantly writing articles about drama in the East and West in *New Youth* (新青年) and *Republican Daily* (in Shanghai, *Chen Zhong Pao* (晨鐘報) and *Gong Yen Pao* (公言報) in Beijing, *Chun Liu* (春柳) and *Xiao Feng* (曉風) in Tian Jing (天津)). During the first half of the twentieth century, the influence of these publications and writers was enormous in Chinese society, where the tradition still entrusted literary intellectuals with tremendous prestige. The two leading trends of literary theory—the Romantic and the Realist—compounded their influences in the Chinese literary circle and stirred up unprecedented discourse during the following centuries of stage drama development in China.

WWII UNTIL 1950

From the Japanese invasion until the end of WWII, the patriotic torrent against foreign aggression stimulated actors, actresses, and dramatic troupes to put on these new stage plays in order to participate in the war in every possible way. These dramatic groups extended their activities to military camps as well as to the far remote countryside. During this period, support for the war effort and depictions of the sufferings of the Chinese people completely overwhelmed people of all walks of life in China. These new stage dramas were always in great demand. The great dramatist Cao Yu (曹禺) produced most plays of that time encompassing social problems such as inequality and the conflicts of all social strata. Even though stage dramas gathered the frustration of the Chinese people and were critical to the establishment, often realistically revealing the dark side of society, they bore the most glorious responsibility of serving the country and against the Japanese invasion.

Moving into the late 1940s, a brief peaceful four years after WWII, stage dramas still captured the passion of theatergoers, even when Western modern cinema was starting to break into Chinese society and reached large audiences. Parallel with the coming of this newcomer, the new stage plays favored episodes of historical dramas and stories reflecting contemporary life. Of this late blooming period, there were *The Secret Volume at the Qin Palace* (清宮秘史), *The Assassination of Emperor Qin* (荊軻刺秦王), and *The Phoenix* (孔雀膽) by Guo Mo-ru (郭沫若) were all popular plays. They were particularly welcomed on college campuses. What was depicted then also was the frustration felt by the Chinese people in another period of complicated social unrest before Communist time, such as was shown in Lao She's *Tea House* (茶舘). Cao Yu's *Sun Rise* (日出) and *Thunderstorm* (雷雨) had fully made use of Western dramatic effects and captured the emotion of the audiences completely. They were good literature insofar as they were shrewd in grasping the frustration of people, but they were said to be politically motivated. On the eve of the ROC's exile to Taiwan in 1949, the rebellious mood of many stage dramas were hushed by the authority and thus their literary scripts were prohibited in Taiwan.

After the 1950s, unfortunately, stage plays did not divorce themselves from sociopolitical functions. Following each social movement promoted by the Communist regime, they became more and more intensely involved in propagandizing political policy and ideology—in this case, Communism. In the Cultural Revolution period, obligatory performances of the officially formulated stage drama, the "Model Beijing Opera (樣板戲)," forced political lectures on Chinese audiences without leaving any space for drama to relate to aesthetic life. Finally, this helped to hasten the collapse of Chinese stage drama. When the mainland once again opened up to the West in the late 1970s, stage drama completely gave way to the rise of a new era of modern cinema.

Conclusive Thought

The advent of stage drama or plays (話劇) in China until its decline on the Chinese stage was short, but indeed complicated in experience. Amazingly, as a lone "foreign good," Western stage drama rode the tide of China's modernization, pounding the beaches of China's port cities and enjoying a sweeping rise. Hand in hand with modern novels, these stage plays were communicated to the general public in the newly thriving literary vernacular and conquered the Chinese stage for at least forty years, not counting what happened after the 1950s. They won applause from audiences all over China, just as wide screen cinema from Hollywood did after the 1950s. The themes and content they tried to portray intimately united the theatre with new trends in liberal thought about marriage and democracy in the beginning but in heavily political propaganda at the end.

In view of their increasing involvement in spreading opinions on social changes and sociopolitical ideas, the stage plays became less and less committed to the purely esthetic qualities of theatrical arts. From an art for art's sake point of view, the troubled Chinese society did not pay much attention to this direction from the very beginning. The Chinese were rather impressed by the social function of the new stage plays and from the very outset perceived them more as tools for propaganda than as independent entities for developing high-quality drama. Certainly, the artistic essence of drama was overrun.

Throughout their life in China, an extremely rough and bumpy existence due to the unrest in society was presented. They enjoyed fame in their formative years with the Spring Willow (春柳社) and Nan Kai clubs (南開). But soon their normal flowering was interrupted as the stage plays plunged into the whirlpool of social movements. Embracing the tide of political and social reforms of each stage, the new drama first helped express the dissatisfaction of Chinese people toward the then-corrupted and weak Qing imperial government and exposed the incompatibility of many social customs. Then, when the effect of the May Fourth Movement in 1919 shattered further the assertiveness of Chinese people to hold their long-standing cultural values and traditions, the new dramas voiced support for progressive social reforms, such as emancipation of the young generation from arranged marriages and careers, and sympathy for women and the poor. The anti-Japanese invasion awakened the theatrical world and the new stage plays communicated full enthusiasm for new drama to join and be the vanguard for its country. After the 1950s, to substitute the public moral education carried by classical Chinese drama, plays were used to campaign for a political ideology, Communism, during the Civil War. In each time period, the new dramas were permeated with the social currents of China, and zealously joined in and performed an active role in them. Stage plays really did not have the time to go through any self-examination of their artistic presentations but became helplessly submerged in and completely dominated by political power struggles. If serious literature cannot avoid reflecting the social trends of its times, the entire history of Chinese stage plays was a manifestation of this experience. Social conflict and turmoil aggravated by foreign invasion (Japan) as well as domestic power strugglers enlisted stage plays as mouthpieces. China and its newly adopted stage drama complemented each other in writing a sad chapter of China's modern history.

Prompted by the advance of electric technology, a brief blossom of the modern movie industry excited Chinese in major cities after WWII. Stage drama reached a decline and soon no longer retained its shining flash on the stages of local theaters. It was after the opening door of China to the West in the 1980s, through the movie industry preserved in Hong Kong, that numerous movies were produced in China. The application of electrified technology on screen was sought to satisfy the general audience for entertainment purposes. The powerful radiance of performance arts on the movie screen replaced the shine of stage dramas. The sway of cinema was so amplified that the professionals and audience for stage dramas have gone to a sweet memorial land. Furthermore, as television became available to every household far and near, television dramas gripped the minds and occupied a large portion of modern-day people's time during daily living at home. Suddenly, world communication had sped up and people were hunting for exotic, foreign cultural tastes. Proper interpretation of foreign traditions became less of a concern and could casually be obstructed. To attract profit by straightly playing on people's emotion and stirring up excitement, ambitious show business produced superficial dramatic films about the cultural traditions of other lands.

When curiosity about China among Westerners increased tremendously in recent years, the ignorance of the general public could easily help someone rocketing into fame with no knowledge of China's cultural and literary traditions. As cinema professionals are increasingly seeking inspiration from Chinese dramas for new products, it is vital for them to gain some proper understanding of China's performing arts, past and present.

NOTES

1. Li, Hong Zhang (李鴻章) (1823–1901), Marques Suyi, Chinese politician, general and diplomat of the Qing Dynasty (1644–1911).
2. Tian, Ben Xiang (田本相), *Comparative Study of Modern Drama History in China* (中國現代比較戲劇史), Culture and Art Publish Company (文化艺术出版社), 1993. P. 27
3. Wang Wei Guo (王衛国). *History of Chinese Stage Play* （中國話劇史）Culture and Art Publish Company (文化艺术出版社) 1998. P. 9.
4. Comparative Study, 3–4.
5. Comparative Study, 9.
6. Comparative Study, 6.
7. Comparative Study, 59.
8. History of Chinese Stage Play, 13.
9. Comparative Study, 10–13.
10. History of Chinese Stage Play, 29–30.
11. Comparative Study, 163.
12. History of Chinese Stage Play.
13. History of Chinese Stage Play, 14–15.
14. History of Chinese Stage Play, 5.
15. Comparative Study, 121.
16. Hu, Xing Liang (胡星亮), Literary Trend of 20th Century Chinese Drama (二十世紀中國戲劇思潮), Research on Drama and Play (戏剧戏曲研究) 1996, Vol. 12, P. 24–26.

Chapter Four

The Dispute over Stage Plays and Traditional Chinese Drama

Tragedy and Comedy

How a drama adapted from another country is viewed and appreciated depends on whether the level of cultural assertiveness on both sides is comparable. Considering the circumstances surrounding the coming of Western stage drama to China, the complex response of the Chinese was not without social and political reasons. Since China was trying to regain its national strength and Western industrialization had conquered China's national imagination, stage drama found an easy entrance to the new land. Looking back at the passionate movement of stage drama, never before in Chinese history had a performing art received such keen attention. The development of stage drama might not have been so favorably accepted without a hitch, if China was on an equal footing with Western powers in terms of social and economic achievement. The extreme criticism toward Chinese opera and the sense of tragedy discussed in this chapter demonstrate the loss of confidence on the part of China. But, Chinese intellectuals would not have disputed the role of drama so ardently if the cultural norms of China had not been so uniquely deep-rooted, yet also so different from those of the West. A balanced exchange between cultures can be reached only when there is a consistent and in-depth search by both cultures to understand the other's background.

When the meeting of two complete strangers—civilizations—takes place, the collision can ignite some extreme expression. The impact of the new on the adopted land usually is stronger and sharper when greater difference exists between two cultural traditions and less significant contact had taken place before. The initial excitement of meeting with each other usually causes some overly excessive and superficial adaptation of one another's cultural characteristics. The interpretation of each other's cultural traditions also tends to be subjectively viewed on the basis of the established values in the minds of the adaptors. The selection of materials is not only scarcely limited but geared to the taste of the adapting culture's background.

In the case of the Western stage play entering China, these characteristics were fully illustrated.

While Western drama and novels were coming, the avalanche of Western influence in all walks of Chinese life was unprecedentedly experienced. The Chinese were shockingly unprepared for the challenge from the West, including the introduction of Western social thought and lifestyle. It was in this desperate mental state that China walked into social reforms and tried to shake away the decayed social traditions. In a totally paranoid manner, some of the May Fourth Movement reformers were so eager to leap forward for modernization that they seriously doubted the sociopolitical cultural establishment of China in the past. The movement excited writers, poets, scholars of social science and philosophy, and educators. Their faulting of the past was so vehement that they saw no trace of anything connecting the old and new—science and technology in particular. This mentality provided fertile land for Western stage drama to set foot in China. In term of literary tradition, the vernacular language movement took the lead in revolt against classical literary works and rushed into the development of the modern Chinese novel and drama that also paved the ways for Western works to set foot on Chinese soil. Despite the then ongoing turmoil and poverty, China's enthusiastic importation of Western drama and novels flooded major cities without obstacles. The philosophical themes and lifestyle in episodes from the Western plays fascinated the minds of educated intellectuals, especially those returned from abroad. When these ideas from a foreign source became caught up in the tidal wave of social reform, they acquired for the new stage play a completely new status as having superior literary quality. Contrary to the soaring popularity of foreign dramas, however, Beijing operatic theatre and folk entertainments were considered to be trivial and platitudinous. They were seen as entertainment for lower social classes by the elite Confucian society for too long to be self-elevated. When the economic condition of the adapting country is weaker, the equality of cultural exchange can never be achieved completely. Chinese drama had to suffer under the downfall conditions in China. The scale of adaptation of each other's tradition between China and the West was definitely not balanced with China on the disadvantaged end.

Rallied by the progressive Western-educated scholars, the urgency of social reform projected that the Chinese theatrical world represented one aspect of backwardness in Chinese life. Modernization had to not only shake off the many corruptions but also disengage itself from the old backward social customs, such as traditional drama. The movement ignited serious self-interrogation among Chinese on their own traditions. The denial of traditional social systems and intellectual thoughts among reform scholars, writers, and poets was widely spread.

However, for thousands of years, China was ruled by a Confucian elite gentry class. They distinguished themselves by their literary accomplishments and their diligence in public affairs. If one knows the influential and powerful force of the Chinese intellectual gentry, one would not be surprised that they, as always, played a role as self-imposed leaders of reform in both political and literary life throughout Chinese history. Therefore, when the new stage drama became a literary topic of interest to scholars, intellectual and social concerns about its development and purpose came to the fore. Intellectuals' various perceptions regarding the conflicting values of Chinese and Western civilizations stirred up among the Chinese waves of disputes. The transplantation of the new drama style into China's cultural environment showed subjective judgement. The integration of the stage plays into Chinese society instigated a furious debate among intellectuals, which led to a renovation movement of the Beijing opera.

For some of the conservative intellectuals, a sense of pride and loyalty among them was induced. The Beijing opera circle raised itself up to take an unyielding stand against the derogatory judgement of progressives. Inspired by the social image enjoyed by the new style of stage drama back in Europe and now in modern Chinese society, a "self-mobilization" movement on behalf of Beijing opera took place. Chinese literary society finally instigated debates over and queries into the value of traditional Chinese drama. Sharp counterarguments were openly presented to the public from the May Fourth movement on. Even though the sparks ignited by the sudden meeting of two civilizations, East and West, broadened the cerebral sphere of China, numerous exchanges on social and cultural ideas erupted fiercely between the Western progressive and Chinese conservative scholars that shook the dramatic circle. To the end, the dispute led to the renovation and survival of traditional Beijing opera and, at the same time, ushered in the fast development of Western style stage play. As the two debating camps wrestled over the respective advantages of the Chinese and the Western dramatic traditions, the artistic value of traditional Chinese opera had taken heed and the question of "tragedy" was raised to challenge the Chinese literary tradition. The waves of passionate discussions elicited about drama illustrated the character of the meeting of two long mutually isolated traditions, Chinese and the Western.

QUESTION REGARDING TRAGEDY

The literary style and effects of Western dramas were given serious consideration by some of the leading scholars and writers. Some were moderate on adoring works from the West but held a reserved attitude in recognizing the unique aesthetic characters of traditional Beijing opera. Qian Xuan-tong (錢玄同) and Liu Ban-nong (劉半農) wrote articles on the underrated performance style and themes of the old Beijing Opera as out of date, unrefined, and vulgar. Hu Shi (胡適), Lu Xun (魯迅), Fu Si-nian (傅斯年), and Zhang Bo-ling (張伯苓) followed.

The substantial introduction of Western literary theory stimulated among Chinese dramatists a particular interest in the relationship between drama, human nature, and society. Two topics emerged to become the center of intellectual concerns, so called "tragedy (悲劇)" and "comedy (喜劇)." The two terms started to appear only when modern vernacular Chinese literary works flourished and the new stage drama (話劇) made its way onto China's stage in the 1920s. As dramatic concepts and genres in Western drama were raised to measure the Chinese dramatic traditions and the mentality of the Chinese people, these two terms started to stir up concerns among Chinese literary intellectuals.

Of all the critical opinion raised by the progressive camp, the question of tragedy was the most shocking and confusing. Some outrageously blunt statements by a group of scholars returning from abroad took precedence, such as whether the Chinese ever developed the genre known as "tragedy." Zhu Guang-qian (朱光潛), for example, the then-influential scholar, concluded in his "Psychology of Tragedy" (悲劇心理學) early in the 1920s that Chinese dramas had neither fully developed "tragedy" (bei ju 悲劇) nor comedy (xi ju 喜劇).[1] He felt that the Chinese lacked resentment over the unjustness of fate and had never recognized that suffering and disasters should be condemned. Thus there was no "tragedy" in China. He actually further concluded that "drama" in China really was synonymous with "comedy" which happened to be coincide with a similar view of French critic, Denis Diderot (杜赫德) stated earlier in the 1700s. Zhu's statement was entirely derived from his knowledge of Western drama theory. His statements, such as "Tragedy exhausts pity and fear by arousing these emotions to their utmost and by providing them with their most perfect objects; it excites concern and directs it into its proper channel," and "it brings the mind into its normal condition by energizing its capacity for painful emotion" had their origin in Aristotle and were very familiar in the West.[2] But these were quite incomprehensible to most Chinese, who had never related this kind of psychology to drama. Additionally, Jiang Guan-yun (蔣觀雲) followed in the same vein and went further by saying that it was a shame that the Chinese performing arts had never developed "tragedy"[3] and was a laughing matter among nations. Theorists such as Xiong Fo-xi (熊佛西), Hong Shen (洪深) and Ma Yan-xiang (馬彥祥), all held dearly to the idea that to strive unyieldingly against fate or unjust treatments and eventually meet one's predestined end is a "tragedy" and Chinese had never had that experience. These well-stated definitions as the basis of their charges against Chinese drama (Beijing opera) can fly beyond drama altogether, touching the human nature of the Chinese.

Stimulated by the publication of books on drama theory, discussions contrasted Western drama traditions in relationship to human nature and society with Chinese traditions. Xiong Fo-xi (熊佛西), the early leading dramatist, for example, studied Brander Matthews's *The Development of Drama* and *The Theory of the Theatre* by American leading dramatist Clayton Hamilton. Xiong's interpretation of the law of the theater, as Matthews puts it, which is that a drama must "deal with an exercise of human will"[4] was that an actor needed to perform in front of the audience on stage applying the power of emotion, not reasoning, to present the conflict of the people's will. Referring to the statement by Aristotle, that "through pity and fear effecting the proper purgation of these emotions," Xiong pointed out that tragedy seeks the proper disclosure of pity and fear, and eventually stirs up sympathy and reverence, such as in *Hamlet*. He gave extensive analysis of action, plot, the ending, and the character of tragedy and concluded that tragedy is the highest form of poetry. Instead of using the Chinese tragedy of *The Injustice Done to Dou e* (竇娥冤), he choose the story of the Song Hero, Yue Fei (岳飛) as example to compare with Shakespeare's *Hamlet* and Ibsen's *Ghosts*. He believed that promotion of performing tragedy would help promote positive qualities in the human race. He was deeply frustrated over the fact that the lack of sympathy among Chinese in the society of his time.

The other theorist, Hong Shen (洪深), integrated opinions of three dramatists, the "The Conflict Theory" by Ferdinand Brunetiere of France (1849–1906), "The Crisis Theory" by William Archer of Britain, and "The Contrast Theory" by American dramatist Hamilton. He added his own interpretation to the three theories: that the drama of conflict demonstrates the most aggressive actions in seeking happiness, drama of crisis presents the most critical occasion that people need to gain happiness, and drama of contrast points out the helplessness of people trying to win happiness. He emphasized that drama should present parts of human life where the future and well-being of human beings would be affected.[5] Dramatist Ma Yan-Xiang (馬彥祥) also referred to the theories of conflict and crises in his *About Drama* (戲劇概論). He dealt with tragedy and comedy. A struggle with fate is a common theme in Greek tragedy, the fault of a person's own character is a common theme in Shakespeare tragedies, and a struggle with the social environment is a theme in Ibsen's modern tragedy. Like Xiong, he was aware of the lack of a substantial definition of comedy from Aristotle's day but gave reference to Aristotle's *Poetics*. He then devoted more effort to the category of comedy: comedy of romance, humor, and satire. He quoted the theory of an Italian writer, Carlo Goldoni, who wrote that in comedy, satire can help correct people's mistakes and a playhouse can be a school that teaches how to prevent these mistakes.[6] Based on T. Hobbes, H. Spencer, and C. R. Darnins' studies, Ma seriously introduced the theory of laughter to the Chinese.[7]

Dramatist Zhang Min (章泯), one of the most thorough theorists in the discourse of Western tragedy, gathered the theories of Barret Clark, F. B. Millett, Friedrich Von Schiller, and Lewis Campbell and others and wrote *Discourse on Tragedy* (悲剧論) and *Discourse on Comedy* (喜剧論). It gave a systematic discussion of the historical development of tragedy in the West and the influence of Aristotle's thought on each period of the history of Western drama. His *Discourse on Comedy* classified comedy into six categories: Greek, Roman, medieval, Victorian, Elizabethan, and Molièrean. His works about tragedy and comedy then aroused a feverish dispute in China.

Zhang Min (章泯), Ma Yan-xiang (馬彥祥), Xiong Fo-xi (熊佛西), and many scholars at that time also made an intensive investigation on drama and concluded that drama is an art composing together literature, music, painting, sculpture, dancing and architecture which laid a significant foundation for the early development of Chinese stage drama from the West.[8] The essence of dramatic theory and the aesthetic value of drama that they studied were drawn mainly from the work of Brunetiere, Archer, Matthews, Schiller, and Hamilton.

Last but not least, Song Chun-fang (宋春訪) was the most accomplished scholar responsible for the introduction of various aspects of Western European drama and theory. He applied his theory of evolution in drama to explain the rise and fall of literary trends, such as the replacement of the Classics with the Romantics. With great effort, he introduced *One Hundred Famous Contemporary Drama* (近世名劇百種目) of Western Europe which enjoyed tremendous popularity among Chinese intellectuals.

When these theorists became more involved in the literary discussions, their attention was directed more forcefully to China's crisis of modernization and reform. Their opinion came in time to share the concern. Xiong Fexi (熊佛西), Hong Shen (洪深), and Zhang Geng (張庚) promoted tragedy and comedy to save China and emphasized the role of drama in social movements. Ma Yan-xiang (馬彥祥) once said that the conflict between capital and labor shown in drama should appeal more attention than that between husband and wife. And the greatness of Ibsen is that he foresaw the coming of social calamity and forewarned the people.[9]

These progressive dramatists also tried to deal with comedy while intensely discussing tragedy. For example, Xiong Fo-xi (熊佛西) rarely passed on an opportunity to eagerly commit to the idea of reform in China. Dwelling extensively on what he believed to be the essential elements of Western drama, he started to accuse his fellow Chinese of lacking sympathy and compassion in his study of tragedy. His invocatory pleas for arousing the Chinese from depression and self-depreciation included not only urging the poets and writers to write for the ignition of the "fire of life (人生的火焰)" among fellow Chinese, but also zealously promoting comedy. He felt strongly that the Chinese had suffered for thousands of years under the bondage of kinship living and had lost the ability to laugh. Restraining themselves in a quiet manner had been too long a habit for the Chinese. They should learn how to burst into a good laugh. His disappointment and frustration over the backwardness of Chinese people and society was so strong that made him believe that the promotion of tragedy and comedy was the most efficient way to save China.

Actually, these theorists were only a few among a large group of enthusiastic intellectuals whose topics were much broader than what is sampled here. Obviously, all of them were among the many returned from study abroad and ardently wanted to introduce anything new to China out of concern for the survival of their country. Under their enthusiastic promotion, the new stage drama flourished because of its realistic life scenario performed in a free style by the cast on stage. Restrained by an established format, traditional Beijing opera was handicapped and at a disadvantage. The freer format of Western theatre amazed the Chinese and the practical function of the theatre to carry out social reform and moral teaching was readily accepted. But the theory of the aesthetic value of drama for illustrating human nature required more comprehensive education for most Chinese.

Unfortunately, their strategic vision on writing essence of dramatic expression and the esthetic value of Western drama went astray and did not appeal to most Chinese as expected. Their theoretic discussions were confined to literary scholars familiar with Western drama and literature. Intending to be insightful, they devoted their dramas to touching upon the intrinsic nature of drama and what drama is to life, its social function and audience. To their disappointment, their eagerness antagonized those local Chinese scholars whose stronghold on Chinese traditions enthused waves of defensive rebuttal. When Chu made his statement that China had no tragedy in drama, he was troubled that the Chinese lacked a progressive spirit on social issues. His announcement was shocking news indeed for most Chinese. Chu and his friend failed to realize that there were basic differences between the Eastern and Western traditions, and drama, as an integral part of its civilization, should be understood accordingly. If a cultural element is to settle in a foreign land, its chance of being accepted would be threatened if a critical or conquering approach to the adaptor's whole civilization is applied. To relate knowledge of Western drama to criticizing and interpreting the expressions of Chinese drama, Beijing opera, was already blunt and harsh. To directly negated the inborn mental ability of Chinese people was a serious mistake. How could people not question that, with the thousands of years of civilization and life experience, Chinese have never had any "tragedy" in their society? Are we saying that the immutable "nature" that is supposedly shared by all human beings excludes the Chinese race? Sure enough, a major protest led by a group of scholars began to deliver their opinion against the progressives.

The question of whether the concepts of Western drama can be applied to comment upon the aesthetic and cultural values of Chinese drama quickly became a topic of discussion. In opposition to Zhu's line of thought, the forerunner scholar and guardian of Chinese classical drama, Wang Guo-wei (王國維), listed a number of traditional Chinese dramas and argued that the Chinese had developed numerous tragedies as early as the Yuan period (1277–1367 AD). To name only a few famous ones, *The Orphan Zhao* (趙氏孤兒), and *The Injustice Done to Dou E* (竇娥冤), all contained major characters who demonstrated the willpower to protest against the unjustness of fate.[10] Of the Kunqu (崑曲) dramas of the Ming period (1386–1644 AD), *The Firmiana Rain* (梧桐雨), *Palace of Longevity* (長生殿), *The Peach Fan* (桃花扇), and *Autumn in Han Palace* (漢宮秋) are all tragic stories beloved by the Chinese. To bluntly inform the Chinese that there was no tragedy in their theatre was almost like telling them that there was no grief or stories with sad endings in their cultural world. Wang was the first to appreciate the theatrical value and aesthetic expression of Chinese drama. His rebuttal was a straightforward voice for understanding Chinese drama from a traditional Chinese point of view without direct reference to the Western theory of drama. When he was claiming that China produced quite a few beiju (悲劇), which fit precisely the "tragedy" defined in the West,[11] he did not argue the point of view from the West.

In view of what is discussed above, it is crucial that arguments interrelating examples of Chinese drama should be critically examined against a broader background. Dramas are closely influenced by their cultural upbringing. Understanding the different style of Eastern and Western drama may be enlightened through discussions of the basic difference between Eastern and Western civilizations.

The following are points of discussion:

1. Philosophical thoughts and cultural attitudes decide the style and subject matter dealt with in literary works, including drama. The origin of difference in expression in Eastern and Western drama is that the West took a metaphysical stand, investigating the relationship between human beings and their environment, whereas the East, at least in China, was concerned with the wellbeing of human beings within the mundane world. Human nature, the

relationship between human beings' and nature, God and nature, and interhuman relationships are all ultimate questions that still need to be answered in Chinese drama. In the world of Western drama, the presentation of conflicts between these elements oftentimes is the subject. For instance, in Greek drama conflict is illustrated when an individual struggles against the power of nature and predestined fate. Tragic conflicts and phenomena were dramatized on stage and taken seriously. Conflict was revealed when one failed to overcome the shortcomings of his or her own character—Shakespearean tragedy, e.g. Othello and Hamlet. Conflict also arose when one person's effort could not break through the set social rules and their power. Conflict existed when idealistic dreams were not rewarded by what was in reality. Constant examination and logical analysis of the definitions of conflict and tragedy were topics for Western theorists but not for Chinese. Contrary to the Western philosophically analytical approach, Chinese drama could be said as developed under a morally judgmental approach. Logical investigations of human nature and philosophical analyses of conflict between humans and the supernatural being or society have not been issues focused on by the Chinese. The struggle to fulfill kindness, righteousness, loyalty, honesty, and chastity in contrast to evil doing, selfishness, greed, and killing are issues concerned in the world of Chinese drama. A real Chinese tragedy (悲劇) can be identified when the ending fails to reward the virtuous and punish the evil after the display of the conflict between positive and negative moral forces. According to Chinese moral traditions, grief, misfortune, or a disastrous ending without a properly answered moral reason is out of the norm. A tragic ending cannot be left simply as predestinated "fate" or phenomena arising from the conflicts of human nature. To reveal the conflicts of human nature is not the intended theme of most Chinese drama. Likewise, the conflicts between individuals and their universal or metaphysical searching is not reflected in Chinese drama.

2. Drama in the East and West had its own unique growth experience which is closely related to their different philosophical background and social traditions. In the West, drama had developed as a literary art together with fiction. Its schemes and plots are structured and somewhat can be evaluated objectively in its own genre. The themes intend to pass messages to or enlighten the audience. With a set definition for development in place at least since Aristotle, drama in the West was given an independent life which rendered a unique style of comedy and tragedy. Scholars and philosophers in the West quite thoroughly analyzed plays according to their form as either "tragedy (悲劇)" or "comedy (喜劇)" and gave sets of definitions to guide the route for dramas' independent development in later ages. An enormous number of plays were written to fulfill the style with plotted narratives and philosophically designed themes. Script writers generally had certain theatrical concepts in mind before plotting a theme to express their views on the

reality of the human world. Western dramatists have attempted to logically classify tragedy and comedy into categories. For instance, some dramatists explain that comedy can be grouped as comedy of romance, humor or satire, and domestic comedy. Where tragedy endows with worth; comedy takes the worth away. But this whole logical approach to define or contemplate the difference between tragedy and comedy has not been a great concern of Chinese dramatists. Under the domination of Confucian social norms, the novel and drama have always been treated as "unworthy small talk." The writing of influential official scholars, such as their poetry, prose, and social and philosophical essays, were considered refined literary works and thus composed the major portion of Chinese literature. Therefore, before Western influence came to China at the turn of the nineteenth century, Chinese dramas were mostly melodramas narrating a series of events, like *The Tale of the Lute* (琵琶記). They often presented stories on stage originating from popular legends and stories by street story-tellers of the old days. Philosophical examination and the illustration of conflicts in social or human nature and structured for a drama were not intentionally developed as a literary style. The rise and fall of drama and performance on stage, from *Yuan za ju* (元雜劇) to Beijing Opera (京戲), was casually left to the entertainment world with some puerile themes. They were not seriously delivered by intellectuals nor did they closely follow social developments.

3. "Tragedy" (悲劇) is used among Chinese to signal a "sad ending event" without awareness of how Greek or Renaissance dramatists defined the term. For Westerners, tragedy is serious and sad, and comedy is amusing and full of levity. In modern Chinese language, comedy (喜劇) simply connotes the concept of a happy ending drama and tragedy (悲劇), on the other hand, denotes calamity with misfortune, grief, or a disastrous ending. Yuan drama developed with a unique structure and format, but with no philosophical definitions to categorize the plays as "tragedy 悲劇" or "comedy 喜劇." *The Injustice Done to Dou E* (竇娥冤) and *The Orphan Zhao* (趙氏孤兒) are great tragic dramas among hundreds that have been favored by the Chinese for centuries. But, traditionally, the Chinese have never singled them out for analysis against a theory of tragedy. It is in vain to try to differentiate the huge number of classical Chinese dramas into "tragedy 悲劇" or "comedy 喜劇" or subjected to the process of philosophical analysis based on Western theoretical definitions.

The theater presents the sorrow of partings and the joy of union that life flouts. It has lured tears and laughter from the Chinese for thousands of years. A great number of Chinese tragedies strike the audience with pity and fear when they watch those who suffer undeserved misfortune on stage. But these feelings are direct human reactions to incidents on stage that people could encounter in life, not necessarily induced by a philosophically designed theme prepossessed by the concept of "tragedy" in the West. Thus,

Chinese drama did not develop under a mold of a concept as either "comedy 喜劇" or "tragedy 悲劇." Statements such as "tragedy exhibits life as directed to important ends; comedy is either not directed to such ends, or unlikely to achieve them"[12] exhibit the typical logical approach in the Western tradition. But Chinese dramatists were never tempted to contemplate drama in this way.

Especially since traditional drama was never given such a lofty position as an art on stage nor important enough to deserve mention by great thinkers, the authors were not given prominent social status nor was their work created in an established literary style. Operatic drama was left as entertainment for commoners and thus consists of grossness of language. Even in the Qing Dynasty, when traditional opera won the favor of the imperial court, it was still considered ludicrous in the eyes of virtuous scholar officials. The Chinese emotion expressed in traditional Chinese dramas certainly could not fit into the definition of "tragedy" in the West.

Therefore, linguistically, while examining the Eastern and Western drama traditions, one will find that the two terms, "bei ju 悲劇" in Chinese and "tragedy" in English do not coincide completely or correspond distinctly in literary meaning. So is the case with comedy and "xi Ju 喜劇." To apply the two modern terms to discuss classic Chinese drama is not appropriate. To translate "tragedy" as understood by the Western tradition with the Chinese term "bei ju 悲劇" shows a lack of consideration of the domain of meaning that the two words cover. The Chinese word 悲劇 (tragedy) stands for tragic events as social phenomena, which people helplessly experience in every society; it can be seen as a sophisticated term denoting calamity. Any misfortune or incident that causes grief or has a disastrous ending is termed a "bei ju 悲劇 (tragedy)" in Chinese. In the world of Chinese literary history, thousands of "bei ju 悲劇 (tragedy)" were written and performed on stage. They are like novels in China that are amusingly written to entertain people and prohibited as serious readings for education, even though the moral education of the general public was unintentional but realistically carried out by traditional drama.

4. From the earliest time in Greece, the tragedy of fate intended to explain the reality of the human world. Ma Yen Xiang (馬彥祥) offered an interpretation by defining "tragedy" in Western drama to the Chinese as the struggle of the human race against fate, their natural shortcomings, and their environment. No matter how hard a person fights in these tragedies, he eventually fails. During the Renaissance, the rise of individualism and self-realization prompted another wave in the creation of drama. Heroes or heroines' individual character were made to stand out more. Characters in these plays meet their fate because of their tragically prophesized personality which tangles with their own complicated responsibilities. With structured plots, some Western dramas seriously illustrated in tragedy that one's own actions serve

as the cause of one's endurance of suffering, not one's circumstances and adversity. This kind of philosophical or analytical approach to human life is the base of Western tragedy, which made tragedy a literary style in Western civilization. Tragedy or comedy in Chinese literature is not preoccupied with authors' grave or lighthearted view on human life. To plot an event for the purpose of "revealing" the characters of an individual in conflict with human nature or their social conditions was not intentionally or systematically developed as a literary style in the world of Chinese drama. This could be rooted in Chinese philosophical traditions that do not lean overwhelmingly on metaphysical or logical concepts but are guided by the ethics of human living to a great degree.

5. The Western dramatist might fictionalize actions to manifest a common denominator of human nature, such as greed, jealousy, or kindness. The scheme may also be designed to be full of accidental circumstances around the action or having prearranged incidents that form the character. Mysterious atmospheres are added for dramatic effects. Ideally, the audience is so moved that questions about human nature are left in their minds upon leaving the theater. The popularly referred to theory that tragedy strikes people's senses so that feeling of pity and fear for one's own fate is aroused must be sourced from this kind of philosophical approach. Thus, that tragedies intend to induce positive educational messages is part of the whole world of Western drama. Whereas, in the case of Chinese dramas, to suffer the consequences of one's own actions is usually caused by one's unethical behavior. A direct chain reaction in which an action is committed against the moral doctrines of Confucian ethics or Buddhist teachings results in punishment. To suffer poverty or physical hardship usually incites incentive for success, like numerous self-made scholars from the gentry experienced through the Civil Examination. There are not many mysterious coincidences ingeniously arranged so that self-awareness is stimulated. For instance, *The Orphan Zhao* (趙氏孤兒) and *The Injustice Done to Dou E* (竇娥冤) are both great "bei ju 悲劇 (tragedy)" in China. The former was translated into several European languages as early as 1734 and attracted great attention in the writers' circle in which the relationship between master and servants as one of kindness and loyalty to each other has always been overwhelmingly praised. At a time when considerable political calamities struck official Zhao's family, Cheng Ying (程嬰), the loyal servant, gave up his own son in exchange for the life of the last Zhao inheritor for the Zhao family's revenge. People were so moved by Cheng's behaviors. Royalty, righteousness, and indignation at injustice exemplified by the servant profoundly signified the Chinese tradition. But never before in China had the audience been led to appreciate tragic elements of drama from the Western point of view, namely that the servant's own actions were the cause of his suffering. Dou E (竇娥), a poor country maid, was accused of murder and executed. At the time when modern stage

drama was in its infancy, literary trends from the West, Romanticism or Realism, were quoted to discuss traditional Chinese drama. In these two Chinese tragic dramas, although ominous circumstances and devious people surrounding the central characters were presented, the servants in *The Orphan Zhao* (趙氏孤兒) and *The Injustice Done to Dou E* (竇娥) persisted in their responsibility to justice. It was their virtue and moral behavior that made them entitled to be hero and heroine of their tragic fate.

DISCUSSION OF SIMILARITY IN EXCEPTIONAL CASES

It is interesting that Wang Guo-Wei (王国維) applied the thought of German philosopher Arthur Schopenhauer to the Chinese tragic style of *The Dream of the Red Chamber*. Schopenhauer said: "The will of human race is a constant blind impulsiveness which cannot be controlled. They pursue the satisfaction of desires which is never ending. Therefore the will of human race itself is the source of sadness. Life is to search how to cut off the desire and then free from its net." As a western philosopher, Schopenhauer was quite a prominent scholar on Buddhist philosophy also. His theory of the will in human nature seeking satisfaction and pursuing uncontrollable desire is what in Buddhism is called worldly desire. But this goal was for the acquiring of happiness in the human world whereas in Buddhism, to cut off desire from the net of the human involvement is for the purpose of relief from worldly suffering and totally detaching from the human world. Wang recognized Schopenhauer's wisdom, but extended it further in Buddhism teaching, writing that "*The Dream of Red Chamber* illustrated the tragedy of life in ordinary moral and family life. It emphasizes the longing for freedom from this secular world (in Buddhism) and is quite contrary from seeking happiness in the human world."[13] The tragic ending of *The Dream of Red Chamber* significantly manifested the impermanence of the human world and how the main character, Bao Yu (寶玉), was freed from dealings with the human world and reached his happiness. Actually, the notion of both Schopenhauer and Wang fails to recognize further that the tragic plot of the novel *The Dream of the Red Chamber* (紅樓夢) reveals many tragic elements similar to Greek drama. The similarity of tragic nature between ancient Greece rites in Greek drama and Buddhist and Taoist legends in the nineteenth-century novel is obvious.

The Dream of the Red Chamber (紅樓夢) was written completely with a Chinese cultural setting and cast with mystery and legends of metaphysical Taoism in the beginning. The legend of a piece of rock left by the Goddess Nyu wa (女媧) was taken to the secular world (紅塵) to experience the cycle of life, a predestinated tragedy according to Buddhism—like a dream through the suffering of birth, old age, sickness, and death. The novel begins with the prophecy of a love tragedy foretold by a Monk. The Sacred Stone was taken by the Daoist priest to enter the cycle of reincarnation and transformed to be the main character Pao Yu (寶玉) in the novel. He suffered extreme sorrow when his love and wishful union with his beloved cousin Dai Yu (黛玉) was severed by a secretly planned wedding to another cousin, Pao Chai (寶釵). Helpless and unable to cope with this family arrangement, he disappears and is nowhere to be found when he discovers the bride was not Dai Yu (黛玉) on the wedding night. Falling in love at first sight, Pao Yu (寶玉) and Dai Yu (黛玉)'s innocent affection was no less than the romance between Romeo and Juliet in early modern Italy. The episodes of the novel have been developed into popular plays on stage. Their tragic effects on the young lovers' fate are so overwhelming that the heartbreaking feeling of pity and fear never fails to win tears from audiences.

If ancient Greek rites are extended in Greek drama, the rituals of Taoist immortals are alive in Chinese novels, such as in *The Dream of Red Chamber*. Pao Yu (寶玉)'s divine love for Dai Yu (黛玉) is a reenactment of what the Stone did in the Palace of the Taoist Jing Huan Fairy (警幻仙子). As the main character in the novel, the Sacred Stone carries out an affair with the reincarnated Fairy of the Red Plant (絳紅草) whom he had nourished sometimes in Taoist Heaven. The Fairy of the Red Plant (絳紅草) was said to vow to return the care of the Sacred Stone with all her tears as she was wondering in the Court of Hatred–Separation (離恨天). This heavenly legend was transformed to a love tale in the mundane world with the Sacred Stone as Pao Yu (寶玉) and the Fairy of the Red Plant (絳紅草) as Dai Yu (黛玉). A secular marriage was not a prearranged event as it was at the ending of the novel, since both the stone and the fairy were destined to return back to Heaven. Their love was never going to end happily in the mundane world, even though it was expressed so passionately and divinely. Dai Yu (黛玉) never failed to shed tears on almost all occasions during her time with the Sacred Stone, Pao Yu (寶玉).

Of *The Injustice Done to Dou E* (竇娥冤) is another example; the drama successfully demonstrates the resentment of a lone young maiden toward the injustice she encounters in her life. The play transforms one woman's fate into a powerful event of conflict in fighting for justice. The supernatural power, Heaven, answers her plea and testifies to her innocence at her death by causing snow in June. The cosmic power takes over when the human world cannot hold itself under the rules of justice. But the drama did not win the attention of reform scholar dramatists because they did not see the characteristics of the drama similar to tragedy under the frame of Western literary theory. No discussion of whether the natural flow of human nature or the behavior of Dou E (竇娥) was responsible for her fate was mentioned. The Chinese accepted it as an extremely sad story, a case of "bei ju (悲劇)".

In conclusion, it was not until the eighteenth century that the coming of Western literature to modern China stimulated the application of Western drama concepts to discuss classical Chinese drama. The Western-educated Chinese scholars of the twentieth century were intellectually fascinated by the whole approach of Western drama, yet emotionally attached to the reform of China. Their critical attitude was formed under an extremely twisted social condition in China—the backwardness of China versus the advancement of the Western countries in industrialization and economics. While growing up in a society where Confucian domination was still strong and the aesthetic and literary values of Chinese drama were not recognized, but left as low-class entertainment, dramatists were overly excited to learn the ways of Western and Greek drama. Their critical statements were based on their perception of "tragedy or comedy" of Western tradition and did not take into consideration the different developmental pattern of the Eastern and Western civilizations. Their Western concepts might be well-known among the re-formers' own circle, but they were hardly far-reaching to the general Chinese population of that time.

As aforementioned, bei Ju (悲劇) or xi ju (喜劇) as Chinese terms do not connote what "tragedy and comedy" signify in Western drama traditions. Therefore, the question of "tragedy" did not arouse counterarguments in theory, but rather social political concern. If, from the beginning, writers were to choose a term other than the Chinese term, bei ju (悲劇), to discuss Western tragedy, such as "xi fang bei ju 西方悲劇 (Western tragedy)," it may be helpful for their communication to people in China. It would not have aroused a bitter attitude toward reform scholars. if Chu Guang-qian (朱光潛) simply stated that xi fang bei ju (西方悲劇) had never existed (or was developed) in China and refrained from an overly strait-laced comparison and unilateral criticism of Chinese drama, then his discussion of traditional Chinese drama based on his perception of "tragedy" or "comedy" of the Western tradition would be more comprehensible.

Actually, the human mind universally acts with the same creative traits, except those traits can be diverted to different paths under different cultural traditions. At times they share the same road, just as *Red Chamber* and Dou E do with some Greek dramas. But largely they each developed undisturbed on their own path, with Chinese cultural tradition casting the dramas and plays into a molded storytelling structure and Western tradition with clearly defined forms of tragedy and comedy.

As a result of the coming of Western drama, the artistic expressions of Beijing opera became the center of attention as a topic of dispute, after this brief encounter of Eastern and Western literary exchange. The two literary dramatic styles really cannot be judged as to which is of better or more sophisticated quality than the other in artistic value. The Western concepts of drama were developed and carried out within the Western tradition, and

China had its own. One has to approach Chinese dramas then as they were produced against their own cultural traditions. Chinese drama's lack of high social status from the early days made them fail to be examined with "theory," even though some of the works are profoundly authored and can stand just as outstandingly as any literary work in global civilizations. Drama in both the East and West has its own great accomplishments. A question of "superior" or "inferior" should not be applied to judge the value of them.

Drama, like many cultural expressions, reflects one side of a unique civilization. Whereas bittersweet dramas have filled the stage in China, well-schemed tragedy and comedy have been cherished by Westerners. The high-pitched singing of female singers in Beijing opera can hardly attract applause from Western audiences; in turn, the soprano of Western opera is jarring to most Chinese. Similarly, dramatic "tragedy" exists in both the East and West: one is structured with philosophical insight and definition and one without. How can one judge which one is more progressive than the other?

NOTES

1. Zhu, Guang qian (朱光潛), *Psychology of Tragedy* (悲劇心理學), People's Literature Publish Company(人民文學出版社), 1982.
2. Elder, Olson. *The Theory of Comedy* Bloomington: Indiana University Press, p. 36.
3. Lan, Fan (蓝凡), Paper of Comparative Study on Eastern and Western Drama (中西戲劇比較論稿件), Xue Lin Publish Company (学林出版社), 1992, P. 545.
4. Brander, Matthews. *The Development of the Drama*, New York: Charles Scribner's Sons, 1912, p. 74.
5. Tian, Ben Xiang (田本相), Comparative Study of Modern Drama History in China (中國現代比較戲劇史), 文化艺术出版社, 1993, P.371-372.
6. *Comparative Study of Modern Drama History in China* (中國現代比較戲劇史), 381.
7. *Comparative Study of Modern Drama History in China* (中國現代比較戲劇史), 382.
8. *Comparative Study of Modern Drama History in China* (中國現代比較戲劇史), 373.
9. *Comparative Study of Modern Drama History in China* (中國現代比較戲劇史), 386.
10. Paper of Comparative Study on Eastern and Western Drama (中西戲劇比較論稿件), P. 546.
11. Paper of Comparative Study on Eastern and Western Drama (中西戲劇比較論稿件), P. 6.
12. Olson, 36.
13. Wang, Guo Wei, Aesthetic and Literary Criticism.

Chapter Five

The Movement toward a National Theatre

Renovation and Survival of the Beijing Opera

Through the discussion of the Western concepts of tragedy (悲劇) and comedy (喜劇) and their differences from those of Chinese drama, the cultural character of Chinese drama has been better clarified. Nonetheless, there is still more to say. While the stage drama gradually flourished in China, the stream of Western influence merged and erupted in greater waves to ignite conflict in China in the performing arts circle. In reaction to the critical attack of the progressives, a national theatre movement was evolved in defense of Beijing opera. With hearty love for drama, not only those dramatists and actors in China, but also a group of overseas students in the U.S. joined their effort to a rejuvenation of Chinese drama. Out of respect for hometown arts, the two forces eventually united and achieved some of their projects.

THE MOVEMENT FOR A NATIONAL THEATRE

The Planting Stage Overseas

Freed from the trammels of the Chinese social environment, a "National Theatre Movement (國劇運動)" was launched by a group of students abroad, mainly in the U.S., in the 1920s. They enthusiastically tried to establish a national theatrical art for China with features of traditional Chinese drama and some principles of Western drama.

Different from the aforementioned reformers, this group of theater lovers also entered the classrooms of the best higher educational institutions in the

West but were well versed in the essence of Chinese literary tradition. They planted the buds of a National Theatre movement for China by having acquired advanced knowledge in theatrical arts. Initiating their activities at Columbia University, Yu Shang-yuan (余上沅) and Wen Yi-duo (聞一多), together with students in the field of drama of other schools, such as Zhang Jia-chou (張嘉儔), Zhao Tai-mou (趙太侔), Xiong Fo-xi (熊佛西), and Gu Yi-qiao (顧一樵) put on a performance of Chinese drama in New York in 1924. Unlike the dramatists of the Spring Willow era, however, they did not perform Western drama in Chinese nor put on plays built around current social issues in China. Rather, they acted out the plots of traditional Chinese dramas with scripts in English.

Aware of the significant position of dramatic arts in Western society, these reformers retained the performing style of Chinese opera and emphasized its literary value to pursue the support of the Chinese American community and successfully staged two dramatic shows, *Reunion of the Immortal Couple* (牛郎織女) and *The Death of the Beloved Queen* (此恨綿綿). Both shows enjoyed enormous success. They used colorful Chinese historical costumes and symbolically designed stage backdrops—both features of Chinese drama—but presented them like Western stage plays without operatic singing. Helped by these theater lovers and their expertise, a Chinese students club in Cambridge, Massachusetts followed their style and produced another play, *The Tale of the Lute* (琵琶記), on March 28, 1924. It was considered the first showcase of Chinese drama to Westerner in the U. S. and was reported on by the *Christian Science Monitor*. A Chinese Drama Reform Club (中華戲劇改進社) then was formed with such members as Liang Si-cheng (梁思成) and Lin Hui-yin (林徽音), the famous architects, and Liang Shi-qiu (梁實秋), the Shakespeare scholars in China. These experiences buoyed their spirits and assured the direction for their future plans—to establish a Beijing Theatrical Arts Center (北京藝術劇院) in China with a performance Hall, classes in drama and acting, a museum, and a journal called *Puppet Magazine* (傀儡雜誌).[1] Excited by their successful experiment in U.S., they made their plan known to Hu Shi (胡適) in China and asked him to invite the *New Moon Magazine* (半月刊) writers to join their effort. Upon Yu Shang-yuan (余上沅)'s return to China in the mid-1920s, he pioneered a plan for a center of performing arts with Zhao Tai-mou (趙太侔) and Xu Zhi-mo (徐志摩). But soon afterwards, they had to give it up because of lacking financial support.

Interestingly to note, this Chinese National Theatre Movement (國劇運動) was inspired by the Irish Theatre Movement of the late 1800s in England. Even their grand plan for a Theatrical Arts Center was intended to copy The Abbey Ireland's National Theatre in England. As students in drama, literature, and arts, Yu Shang-yuan (余上沅) and his followers must have learned how the Council of National Literary Society and the Literary Theatre closely worked together to raise the literary quality of drama activities in England. The Irish expatriate playwrights "merged their national heritage with the literary heritage of Europe; not only enriching and enlarging that heritage," but elevating the quality of England's theatrical world.[2] The Irish success must have deeply influenced the Chinese students. Just as W. B. Yeats, John M. Synge, and Lady Augusta Gregory worked for an Irish drama renaissance in England, these Chinese intellectuals were sincere about creating a national theatre for China with features identifying it with the unique characteristics of the Chinese people and their traditions. They intended to demonstrate the consciousness of their nation and expand it to match a global standard.

Growing Time in China

The plans for the Chinese National Theatre Movement gradually materialized after Yu Shang-yuan (余上沅) and Zhao Tai-mao (趙太侔) returned to Beijing in the summer of 1925. Focused on the aesthetics of drama, they founded a drama department in the National Beijing Arts Institute (北京國立藝術專門學校) and, to fulfill his dream in drama, Yu opened drama theory and acting classes. Owing to Yu and his followers' passionate and idealistic visionary efforts, Yuan drama was offered as a course at Beijing University despite the opposition from some of the conservative Confucian gentry in society.[3] Soon afterward, Beijing opera was added into the curriculum. These unusual initiatives by an academic institution greatly lifted the social status of traditional Chinese drama. Ignoring the contemptuous attitudes of Confucian gentry as well as criticism from the pro-Western intellectuals, Yu and Zhao joined the mission of local conservationists in starting to renovate classical Chinese drama. A great leap forward for the traditional drama took place when the National Theatre Movement was heralded by the publication of a Drama Section of the Morning News, Chen Bao (晨報). Most articles and books written at that time contained new ideas about drama, as, for example, "Evaluation of Traditional Drama (舊戲評價)" and "National Theatre Movement (國劇運動)" by Yu Shang-yuan (余上沅), Wen Yi-duo (聞一多)'s "The Wrong Path of Traditional Drama (舊劇的歧途)," Zhao Tai-mou (趙太侔)'s "Classical Drama (國劇)," Xu Shi-mo (徐志摩)'s "The Founding of Drama Journal (劇刊始業)," "National Theatre Movement (國劇運動)," etc. A collection of these articles was published by the New Moon Press in 1927.

Attempting, on the one hand, to establish a unique theatrical art representing Chinese tradition, they clung to Beijing opera as a basis of dramatic expression. On the other hand, well versed as they were with Western drama traditions, they were broadminded enough to fully recognize the excessive enthusiasm of the progressive camp for promoting the new Western style stage plays. This National Theatre Movement (國劇運動) took an independent position from the very beginning. Its adherents tried to distance themselves from the debate and chose to view the Chinese opera style as a purely artistic entity, not as crude and vulgar. Their stand was not as totally critical of Chinese drama as that of the pro-Western progressive camp nor was it as inflexible as that of the ultra conservatives, who held that Beijing opera was unchangeable. They wanted to apply the principles of Western drama to traditional Chinese opera in order to create a new style with reformed singing, acting, and stage design called "National Theatre" (國劇). They truly believed that the symbolic and impressionistic characters of Chinese classic drama are profound features that distinguishing Chinese drama from other forms of drama. But a new style of acting would have to be developed for the new theater. For their plans, a great musician, like a Chinese Wagner, would be needed to write new music.

However, during their search for reform, they first had difficulties defining the direction of the dramatic themes. Should the hypothetical production remain "arts for arts' sake," reflecting life merely on the philosophically level, or should it minutely expose the current "realities of life?" Should drama, as a form of artistic expression, also conduct insightful criticisms of life? If drama devoted too much effort to depicting social problems, there would no aesthetic left for drama. Actually, in the beginning, Yu Shang-yuan (余上沅) and his followers pleaded for changing Chinese opera through a reform process that would create a new performance arts form suited to the Chinese tradition, not mingled with social movements. During the process, the prolonged Confucian social tradition caused conservatives to act out by canceling the Chinese opera class and thereby not allowing the reformers to elevate the social stature of classic drama. Unexpectedly, their daring initiative of offering classes on artistic forms of traditional dramas became the target of criticism from both the pro-West progressive camp and some conservative elite scholars. They were accused of promoting coarse and decadent "Old Opera" in the lofty "elite halls" of the higher educational institutions. The magnitude of the influence from the West was so great that young progressive generations turned their back on traditional drama and embraced the new stage plays. Committed to revolutionary reform, the "New Youth (新青年)" writers assailed the "arts for arts' sake" new group as having a highbrow disregard for ongoing social problems of the masses. Before Yu Shang-yuan (余上沅)'s early effort could possibly lead to a trial of his plan, a new form of drama, his idea to set up a National Theatre with Zhao Tai-mou (趙太侔) flickered out within a little more than a year. They recognized the fact that they were too idealistic to reach and influence the greater population and failed in what they had planned. Nevertheless, as one of the purest dramatists with the least concern for sociopolitical reform, Yu continued to promote the study of drama, Eastern and Western, when he was able to establish his own theatrical institution in a later time during and after the

WWII in Nanjing (南京). He continued writing articles expounding his National Theatre Movement (國劇運動).

In view of the short life of this movement, unfortunately, the dedicated efforts by this handful dramatists and writers were dissolved like a drop of clear water in a puddle of mud. Their dream of creating a new art form did not excite people in China, though it was successfully overseas. Maybe the differences between the Eastern and Western drama world, in terms of formats, plots, and themes of social and historical traditions, were so vast that any attempt to merge a new drama style with traditional opera features faced insurmountable hurdles and was destined to suffer failure. In spite of the dedicated effort to merge the two traditions by means of the National Theatre movement, they find the existence of parallel twin tracks of drama serving to entertain the Chinese in the early Republican time, e.g. the "East is East" of Beijing opera and the "West is West" of stage plays. Eventually, as the Western style stage drama fondly embraced the vernacular language stage, the totality of traditional drama's artistic performing style survived without adopting any such Western features.

But, the attempt to establish a National Theater tremendously inspired the future development of Beijing Opera. The group of scholars devoted to this mission was more idealistic than most social reformers. They resented the claim that Chinese tradition was losing its grip. Even though they were troubled by that a sense of inferiority growing among the Chinese, the low social status of a supposedly national theatre (Beijing opera), and loathed the uncouth customs surrounding it, they insisted that their ideal national theater should be one evolved from the traditional Chinese opera in the way they wished. In reality, their national theatre, if patterned after the Western stage plays and shorn of singing and acting, would be what was developed later as "Ancient Customs plays古裝戲." They failed to realize that lyric singing and symbolic gestures are the most unique elements that make up the Beijing opera. Without these basic traditional characteristics and feathers, their "ideal National theatre" would have completely lost its identity as Chinese drama.

They did not conduct a thorough examination of the circumstances that made them successful in the U.S. but not necessarily in China. Far distanced from China, their plays were profoundly appreciated, because the Chinese community in the U.S and Americans around college campuses rarely had a chance to see an authentic traditionally-styled Chinese drama. Plus, the plays were creative and presented with all the features of Beijing opera though the lyric singing was in English and styled actions were simplified. These modifications made their plays quite comprehensible to people who were not familiar with Beijing opera. Whereas in China, the audiences were so well versed with all kinds of Chinese dramas and most of the theatre goers attained their enjoyment particularly by listening to the lyric singing with highly critical standards. The overseas National Theatre's production could not offer anything new to the local Chinese and thus lost its unique status.

Inspired by the Irish movement, Yu Shang yuan (余上沅) and his followers also failed to realize that the Irish movement by nature and circumstance was different from what they were trying to establish in China. When John M Synge and Lady Augusta Gregory were promoting the Irish Renaissance of drama in England, the theatrical art in England was getting monotonous in variety. Irish folk culture, a variety of the British cultural tradition, came in time to characterize and embellish the plays. The format and concept of drama did not deviate from the Western tradition. Irish culture was not completely foreign to people in England as Western culture was to China in the 1920s. Therefore, the Irish movement in drama was to rehabilitate the long inaccessible Irish culture into England theatre. Whereas in China, the National Theatre Movement promoted by the group from the U.S. did not bring in any minor or minority Chinese culture to energize the original settled Beijing opera or help lift its social status. The format and concept of Western drama touched by Irish culture was not equivalent to what these students tried to institute in Beijing Opera. It could not serve the purpose to apply them to Beijing opera as Irish culture applied to England theatre art. Thus, as a result, Chinese stage plays directly inherited the imported Western drama and grew independently from the traditional Chinese drama. Beijing opera had to wait for the passion of its patriotic patron inside China to be translated into a movement capable of being sustained over the avalanche of Western-influenced criticism.

THE MOVEMENT OF RENOVATION INSIDE CHINA

Even with both drama styles entertaining their own audience, feverish and heated debate between pro-Western progressive intellectuals and Chinese conservative scholars was still quite flammable.

The Fervent Debate on the Artistic Value of Chinese Drama

Excited by the new style and theory of Western drama and infatuated with Western literary works, the progressive camp led by well-known scholars launched a critical attack on traditional Chinese theatre and drama through articles published in the *New Youth Journal* (新青年) in 1917. Besides concepts of tragedy and comedy, they subjected to sharp criticism almost all the artistic values and characteristic forms of Beijing Opera, such as the painted face (臉譜), the self-introduction, the singing, and the acrobatics. The pro-Western dramatists firmly committed themselves to installing the new Western style drama in China and refused to acknowledge that the traditional Beijing opera was also sophisticated in genre features and deserve to be called the "national theatre" of China.

In addition to what was discussed in the previous chapter, there was literature that directly criticized Beijing Opera. Qian Xuan-tong (錢玄同) spearheaded the attack by referring to what was campaigned by Hu Shi (胡適) and promoted by Chen Du-xiu (陳獨秀)—that by means of vernacular wording, true feelings and thought would be easier and better expressed. He felt that the semi-classical language and lyrics features of Beijing opera were unable to excite people's true emotions and thought. Liu Ban-nong (劉半農) followed with "My Opinion on Literary Reform" (我的文學改良觀) and sharply criticized all the features of Beijing Opera.[4] Prompted by his zeal for the vernacular literature movement, Hu Shi (胡適) joined the camp and published a potent article, "The Progressive Concept of Literature and Reform of Drama" (文學進化觀念與戲劇改良論).[5] He concurred with most of the points raised by the *New Youth Journal* (新青年) and suggested putting Greek Drama on stage to replace Chinese drama. The points were: first, that literary works (literature and drama) had to keep pace with progress and social development. The edification of ethical states of mind (morals) and emotions as conducted in classical Chinese opera was lacking in progressive thinking. Secondly, that the artistic forms of Chinese traditional drama were only partially developed. The painted faces, the symbolic gestures, and the unreal stage arrangements were mostly inherited from the old and decayed traditions, and were inferior features contestants that should be totally eliminated. Thirdly, that the orchestra and singing, speaking lines, and acrobatics were heterogeneous elements presented together on a single stage. This was backwards as compared with modern drama. Fourthly, the quality of the literary elements and expressions were of vulgar and low taste. As for the dramatic plots, the tales in traditional drama were loosely structured and lacked clear climaxes and fodder for psychological analysis. And most of all, the Western-educated fashioned scholars wanted Chinese opera to abandon its singing aspect and adopt the features of Western stage plays with vernacular dialogues and free action.

These articles provoked furious resentment from the conservatives and at once lit up the flames of opposition. Scholars aligned against the progressives, they soon formed their own camp bravely voicing their opinions with equally powerful defenses. These advocates of native Chinese culture mounted a strong resistance against the overwhelming tide of literary westernization and the condemnations of Chinese opera. Zhang Hou-zai (張厚載), Fang chen (芳塵), and Mr. Ma Er (馬二先生) at once joined forces as the leading few in the battle against the reformers. They took a reactionary view and insisted on preserving the totality of the art of classical opera as it had always been.

Zhang Hou-zai (張厚載), in his *My View on Traditional Chinese Opera* (我的中國舊戲觀) gave a systematic analysis of the art of classic Chinese opera. In particular, he defended the special features of traditional opera stating that the music, singing, painted faces, and acrobatics were unique to and genuinely developed in China only, and that there were definite rules for the composition and combination of all these features when performed on stage. He and his colleagues, Yun Tie-qiao (惲鐵樵), Jiang Zhao-xie (蔣兆燮), and Yan Du-he (嚴獨鶴) repeatedly stated that the symbolic performances of Chinese opera were able to vividly evoke a great many scenes and events in the imaginations of the audience, and that the sentimental lyrics, closely combined with Chinese music, could not be equaled by plain vernacular dialogue in terms of touching the cord of human emotion.[6] In reaction to such extremist opinions as *On the Abandonment of Traditional Drama* by Zhou Zuo-ren (周作人),[7] Zhang Hou-Zai (張厚載) also wrote *Painted Face and Acrobatics* (臉譜, 打把子) and *Modern Literature and Traditional Chinese Opera* (新文學及中國舊戲).[8] His conclusion was that the Beijing opera was a jewel that had found profound development in Chinese society and that suited the traditional environment. It only needed to be preserved—not reformed or improved.

The dispute drew tremendous attention from the public as major newspapers and journals all over the nation were seriously engaged in reporting and discussing the arguments. Among the major participating public press media were The *Morning Bell News* (晨鐘報) and *Public Opinion* (公言報) in Beijing, *Spring Willow* (春柳) and *College Press of Nan-Kai University* (南開, 校風) in Tianjing (天津), and *Public News* (時事新報) and *Petition News* (訟報) in Shanghai.[9] Spearheading the movement, *The New Youth* (新青年) invited both camps to participate in a special edition on the reform of drama (戲劇改良專號) and brought the dispute to a close in October of 1918. Besides Hu Shi (胡適)'s article, there were *All Aspects of Drama Reform* (戲劇改良各面觀) and *Again on Reform of Drama* (再論戲劇改良) by Fu Si-nian (傅思年),[10] Zhang Hou-zai (張厚載)'s *My View on Traditional Chinese Opera* (我的中國舊戲觀),[11] Ou Yang yu-qian (歐陽予倩)'s *My Opinion on the Reform of Drama* (予之戲劇改良觀),[12] and *On Modern Literature and Traditional Chinese Drama* (新文學及中國舊戲) by Chen Du-xiu (陳獨秀). Also included was *An Introductory List of One Hundred European Dramas* (近世名戲百種目) by Song Chun-Fang (宋春舫). One other article published by the New Youth (新青年) later was *Traditional Chinese Drama Should Be Abandoned* (中國舊戲之應廢) by Zhou Zuo-Ren (周作人), after which the conservatives and progressive camp came to a truce.

The Renovation and Survival of Traditional Chinese Drama

To counter the critical attitude of reformer dramatists and in defense of the artistic value of traditional dramas, the conservationists of Beijing opera in China started to gather their strength for a process of renovation that would determine its very survival. Instead of letting Chinese theatre plunge into rapid decline, they launched a "self-examination" of the artistic value of Beijing opera. The attack of the New Youth group (新青年派) was not the sole cause igniting the renovation of traditional drama. In some ways, it was true that the traditional drama or the Beijing opera brought a lot of the criticism upon itself. Up to the end of the Qing period, every conceivable social illness had penetrated deeply in the Chinese traditional opera and theater. It was a sad scene surrounding the entertainment business. Their self-awareness and criticism were quite thorough.

Firstly, as explained previously, having been despised by the elitist literary tradition for thousands of years, actors and actresses in the theatrical profession had never been treated as artists, but as entertainers of lowly social status in Chinese society. At the time when the May Fourth Movement was leading the reexamination of all Chinese social values, traditional Chinese theatre existed and flourished in the most decadent, corrupt, and uneducated social circles. To cater to the tastes of their audiences, most of these traditional performances contained coarse and distasteful dialogues. This type of theater itself appealed only to poverty-stricken families who could not afford to educate their children for public work, in official domains, or in any respectable trade.

Secondly, Beijing opera imposed extremely difficult training on aspiring performers. To attain perfection, they had to endure extreme hardship mastering the music, acting, lyrics of the entire play. Vigorous physical training and personal discipline to perform the martial arts are also required. Yet, their efforts were not generally recognized and rewarded as artistic presentation.

Thirdly, the set format of the acting, highly stylized music and singing, the limited roles of the cast, and the conventional repertoire of historical and folk tales, all handicapped the drama in terms of establishing free communication with the audience and addressing current social issues. While the social movements in China demanded that drama give more voice to such issues as seeking freedom from family arranged marriages or fighting for a democratic political system, the traditional theatre remained helpless, making it completely out of touch with current affairs. Additionally, with modern music flooded into China and changing social scenes, traditional opera could no longer attract talent and imagination to devising plots and composing music and lyres. A new form of drama was waiting to set foot in China.

Amidst all these events, the group that stood for the conservation of traditional Beijing opera believed firmly in their mission. Some held to a liberal view avoiding direct collision with the progressive camp and at the same time, insisted upon preserving the traditional drama features, especially in the singing aspect. They were fully aware of the fact that the many features of traditional theatre had been established for historical dramatic plots and could not fit in with modern themes. The acting, costumes, singing, and spoken lines are so permanently fixed in set patterns and musical tones that they were naturally unsuited for depicting contemporary social movements. Furthermore, over a hundred repertoires of historical events and classical tales already constituted an enormous volume of scripts for the traditional theater. The traditional dramas, like Western operas, were pieces of well-crafted antiques completed for an audience to appreciate. Beijing opera performers also would spend years studying the music and lyrics before they were able to deliver a drama piece.

The advantage of modern Chinese stage dramas on the other hand, was that their performance has no restraints of any kind. They resembled Western stage plays and their acting was executed with naturalistic delivery. They should have their own style advanced and performed for their audience without having to compete with the Beijing opera. Since the conservatives cared more for the aesthetic aspects of theatrical art, they acquired a vision of global coexistence of all forms of theater. Yu Shang-yuan (余上沅) and Zhao Tai-mou (趙太侔) joined Qi Ru-shan (齊如山), Ou Yang Yu-qian (歐陽予倩), Song Chun-fan (宋春舫) and Zhou Jian-yun (周劍雲) in starting a renovation movement in Beijing opera intended to restructure the fragmented scenes and remove the vulgar and uncouth aspects of traditional drama. Experienced the dispute with new stage plays, and inspired by the challenges presented by Western drama art, the conservative camp had surprisingly come out with rebuttals that displayed the artistic quality of Beijing opera. This in itself stimulated a genuine interest among Chinese intellectuals for becoming aware of, and eventually accepting, the artistic status of Chinese traditional dramas.

After years of effort by these dramatists, Beijing opera survived with its original art forms and shook off its many coarse and depraved conventions. Inspired by Western drama, the many smutty acts or expressions in traditional opera have been extracted from modern performance. This early development paved the way for Beijing opera to be ushered into the grand hall of higher education in the 1920s. The first glorious moment that the traditional drama ever enjoyed in Chinese history was when its form and acting were presented in courses at the newly established Beijing Theatrical Arts Institute (北京國立藝術專門學校) in 1925.[13] Later in the 1980s, when the refreshed original style of Beijing Opera was reinstalled in Chinese theaters after the politically twisted and officially formulated stage drama, the "Model Beijing

Opera (樣板戲)," was abandoned, this early renovation effort showed its profoundness again. Today, it has won the appreciation of new generations and has redefined its social status as national theater (國劇). It is interesting to note that as Chinese stage drama was gradually replaced by cinema, there was a traditional opera revival using the modern high technology on movie screens today. The new stage drama had its heyday during the enthusiasm for taking social responsibility, but it has been short lived in comparison with traditional Chinese dramas. It is generally recognized now that traditional Chinese opera is an art form produced in a time period when China was totally saturated in its own traditions. It belongs to its own time and has its own pattern of development and should not necessarily be replaced by a new dramatic form. Like Western opera, its artistic forms and trained skills are highly valued. It has risen from what was referred to as low class entertainments to the position of national opera (both Beijing opera and Kun drama). It has captured a different audience and acquired a higher social status.

As classical theatrical products, if not because of its many decayed feature and the meeting of high tide of Western civilization, they should be left alone from the feverish development of stage drama. The raising of the question of "tragedy" bears a similar phenomenal nature. The style of traditional drama, such as Kun drama and Beijing opera, as it has survived, is more comparable with Western opera combined with Shakespearean or classical Greek drama. Indeed, it is not possible to judge which of the two literary dramatic styles—stage plays and Beijing opera (or Kun drama) is more sophisticated than the other in terms of artistic value.

Compounded by domestic unrest and disastrous wars, the avalanche of Western literature and drama coming into China in the first half of the twentieth century triggered unforeseen changes in Chinese intellectual life. The sharp contentions over the artistic value of China's traditional drama, which led to its final renovation and survival, have been most fascinating.

DISCUSSION

1. As one examines the dispute, it becomes clear that the entire process reflects the complexity of the intellectual movement during a critical historical period in China. The movement was not a literary evolution within China's own tradition but involved social and literary changes drastically incited by the coming of Western civilizations. If one expects the adoption of a foreign literary element to result in a work of new composite form of drama in China, one has to admit that this did not happen in the case of new stage plays and Chinese traditional drama (Beijing opera). Although the unavoidable entry of Western drama and novels into China eventually enriched the modern Chinese performance arts, it did not achieve what the Irish play-

wrights did in England. The two theatrical arts co-existed and each retained its own dramatic features. The exciting experience of the dispute was not caused simply by just the collision of Eastern and Western traditions, but also the sociopolitical conditions of China.

2. An exploration and study of the causes of the dispute show that the motives and opinions expressed by the progressives carried more passion for sociopolitical reform than for drama itself. From Liang Qi-chao (梁起超) to Qian Xuan-tong (錢玄同), Zhu Guang-qian (朱光潛), and Hu Shi (胡適), they were committed to carry on the baton of duty for the future of China. They inherited the elite-gentry tradition, in which the life of intellectuals encompassed both literary and sociopolitical responsibility. When the new stage drama became a topic of the literary arts, they became overwhelmingly concerned with the social function of the performing arts and undertook the mission to modernize the mentality of the Chinese people by means of drama. They took their intellectual and social concerns for the content of the new literary drama as the key to their social movements. Thus, their criticisms had more to do with the survival of China than the aesthetic value of drama.

3. Most of the leading reform scholars were from prominent, educated elite families and the selected few who went to the West for an education had little chance to become familiar with the art of traditional drama (Beijing opera). Even though most of them were well educated in the Chinese classics and traditional Chinese literature before they went abroad, they were, thanks to their elders' good intentions, deprived of exposure to the world of drama, since traditional Chinese theaters were not considered a healthy place for youngsters then. In a morally strict Confucian society, a liking of the music and acting in the entertainment world usually was not nourished in children of educated families. In fact, if not for the coming of the Western literature and drama that ignited a self-evaluation of China's own literary tradition, intellectuals might not have become involved with the debate. Their minds were supposed to be dwelling in philosophical or artistic insights in life or on sociopolitical issues.

Upon their return, these leading reformers were portrayed as academics. During their time, their outstanding education both in China and the West could be in any field but drama. Many of them, such as Qian Xuan-tong (錢玄同), Hu Shi (胡適), Chen Du-xiu (陳獨秀), Lu Xun (魯迅), Liu Ban-nong (劉半農), and Fu Si-nian (傅思年), were, as a whole, really quite naïve about what elements in traditional drama should be despised. They had no concept of how and from where the traditional drama should start transforming itself into a modern literary entity. All they came in contact was the coarse and obscene stories presented in Beijing opera. When Chu made his statement that China had no tragedy in its drama, he was deeply troubled by the Chinese mentality of accepting adversity without seeking alternatives. As one of a few scholars who had studied in England and France and gained the highest academic degrees in the field of literature and aesthetics, his main scholarly achievements were not in the field of drama. In fact, Chu wrote articles and books on a wide range of topics. Hu Shi (胡適) studied philosophy at Columbia University and devoted his early scholarly life to the Vernacular Movement (白話文運動) in China and remained as a leading academician in Chinese history and philosophy. He did express interest in reexamining and reaffirming the literary value of traditional drama, Yuan Drama (元曲), in Chinese history, but not for the sake of praising the dramatic aesthetic effects of modern day Beijing opera. One of the main concerns of prominent reformers like Qian Xuan-tong (錢玄同) and Fu Si-nian (傅思年) was with the reform of Chinese language. They felt that writing with Chinese characters was not efficient enough to cope with the speed of communication in a modern society. Their extreme zeal for embracing new ideas and Western thought against traditional Chinese literary traditions make us doubt that they would even admit that Chinese dramas, such as *The Injustice Done to Dou E* (竇娥冤) or *The Orphan Zhao* (趙氏孤兒) had any aesthetic or dramatic value at all.

4. Of the New Youth group (新青年派), those few scholars who were seriously devoted to the study of drama, such as Xiong Fo-xi (熊佛西) and Hong Shen (洪深), also based their critical views mostly upon their admiration of Western drama. The relevance of the deeply-rooted sentiment of traditional drama in the life of Chinese people was overlooked. The New Youth group was not aware that their critical attitude toward traditional Chinese drama stemmed from the difference of social class in which the theatrical worlds of China and the West were rooted. Dazzled as they were by the new world of Western drama, they completely disregarded the fact that Chinese opera was an art that belonged to its own time and could not be renovated to deal with the evolution of contemporary social conditions. This could be the very reason that the traditional Beijing opera survived and went on entertaining the Chinese people side by side with the new Chinese stage drama until today.

5. Actually, both the progressive and the conservative camps were experiencing a conflict in their self-evolution. For the progressive camp, their study abroad broadened their vision on sociopolitical issues and also deepened their awareness of the backwardness of China. They were experiencing a conflict between extreme opposition to Western aggression and extreme approbation of Western reform. Their eagerness to modernize China upon returning home made them critical of their own tradition and their fellow Chinese. For the conservative camp, they were also fully aware of the indecent customs in the world of Chinese theatre at that time. Yet, for the sake of patriotism to Chinese traditions, they stepped forward to defend the artistic values of Beijing opera. But their intention attracted much criticism and they

endured attacks from the opposition because of Beijing opera's social class. Nevertheless, when the urgency arose for saving China from possible colonization by the Western powers after the First World War, Chinese intellectuals of both camps eagerly joined the surging tide of the May Fourth Movement—a movement that ignited denial of most traditional Chinese cultural values for the sake of modernizing China. This produced a mixed negative attitude toward Western political powers as well as toward China's own traditions—an attitude that threw the Chinese into a whirlpool of confusion lasting until this day.

6. As stated before, any society, when a culture remains inward within its own framework of tradition too long, it needs challenge from other civilizations to break its monotonous situation.

The challenge presented by Western drama and literature to the mentality behind Chinese literary and performing arts erupted in self-examination among the Chinese intellectuals. As a result, not only was the stage play found in China, but also the renovation and elevation of Beijing opera in aesthetic value as well as social status was achieved. But there is a prerequisite condition in which the cultural element to be challenged required being as equally sophisticated and well-developed as the challenger. Otherwise, it could easily be diminished. Pro-Western intellectuals' faulting of the dramatic value of traditional Chinese drama, which triggered an impassioned self-evaluation of the artistic values of Beijing opera among some scholars, was a healthy challenge.

The survival of Beijing opera was not a product of Chinese nationalism, but the demonstration of China's own artistic and literary strength in guarding its survival. Western drama's effective presentation of complicated plots without resorting to the audience's imaginations was required by the conventional acting or stage settings in Beijing opera. Western drama, then, gave Beijing opera a sharp test. But its coming and leaving the stage in China did not uproot traditional Chinese drama.

CONCLUSION

Like most cases, the introduction of a new literary style usually stirs up dispute over the characteristics of a traditional literature of similar style in the initial stage. A self-defensive movement to conserve and reinstate the values of the traditional literary style will probably always rise up against an overly enthusiastic effort to usher in the new style. A new literary style would not have been accepted in a society like China, where a native cultural and literary tradition has been well developed and deeply settled for thousands of years, unless special social conditions had been present.

It is quite understandable that it was the worsened social conditions in China that made the new stage drama able to enter the current of political and social reform, espouse a purpose, and join the mainstream of each social movement as a powerful public medium. Riding the tide of the vernacular language movement, actors and actresses could convey a dramatic tale with expressions from everyday spoken language

Today, amidst all the upheavals and social changes, Chinese traditional drama has not only survived, but has also refreshed its beauty in a modernized society. The bitter arguments that had ensued in literary circles between the conservative camp and the progressive camp was in vain. Few people ever remarked that the development of Eastern and Western drama each had their own patterns and values in terms of their social and cultural environments and thus should entertain the Chinese together.

If some of the early pro-Western critics were living today, they would probably not be so critical of traditional Chinese drama. A long-rooted cultural tradition can survive if given a little nutrition and can also evolve into a superior form, such as in the renovated modern version of the Kun drama *Peony Pavilion* (牡丹亭). A balanced reform of any social or cultural tradition cannot proceed on the basis of complete denial of its roots or blind acceptance of a new foreign element. Had Hu Shi (胡適) and Fu Si-nian (傅斯年) ever imagined that well-mannered Chinese audience would be watching Chinese opera one day in well-appointed theaters, they would have regret for their condemnation of the aesthetic value of Chinese drama. Qian Xuan-tong (錢玄同) would not have vowed to change the Chinese language into an all-phonetic writing had he realized that Chinese characters are an essential element in signaling the meanings and nuances of the Chinese language. Zhu Guang-qian (朱光潛) would shake hands with Wang guo-wei (王國維) in agreement that in many cases "East has to stay East" and "West stay West" as far as literary arts are concerned. There is no point in dickering and debating over which tradition is superior to the other. Lectures on both Eastern and Western traditions in drama can be harmoniously presented in the same university for students. How dull and monotonous would life be if only one uniformed culture is prepared for all people in the human world.

NOTES

1. Yu Shang-Yuan (余上沅). *National Theater Movement* (國劇運動). Shanghai: Shanghai Book Store, 1992.

2. Hunt, Hugh, *The Abbey Ireland's National Theatre, 1904–1978,* New York: Columbia University Press, 1979, P. 2.

3. Tian, Ben Xiang (田本相), *Comparative Study of Modern Drama History in China* (中國現代比較戲劇史), Culture and Art Publish Company (文化艺术出版社), 1993, P.273.

4. Please change this note to "Hu, Xing Liang (胡星亮), *Literary Trend of 20th Century Chinese Drama* (二十世紀中國戲劇思潮), Research on Drama and Play (戏剧戏曲研究) 1996，P.71-72.

5. Ouyang, Zhesheng (欧阳哲生) ed. Collected Essays of Hu Shi, Volume 2, (胡適文集, 第二集). Beijing: Beijing University Press, 1998. Originally published in *New Youth* (October 1918) Volume 5, Number 4 (原載新青年, 第五卷第四號, 1918年10月).

6. Hu, Xing-Liang (胡星亮). *Literary Trend of 20th Century Chinese Drama* (二十世紀中國戲劇思潮), Research on Drama and Play (戏剧戏曲研究) 1996，P. 73

7. *New Youth* 新青年 5, Ch. 4 (1918).

8. *New Youth* 新青年 4, Ch. 6 (1918).

9. Hu, Xing-Liang (胡星亮). *Literary Trend of 20th Century Chinese Drama* (二十世紀中國戲劇思潮), Research on Drama and Play (戏剧戏曲研究) 1996, P. 75.

10. Zhao, Jia Bi (趙家璧) ed. Collections of Modern Chinese Literature: Theory of Development, by Hu Shi (胡適), Shang Hai Good Friend Publish Company (上海良友图书印刷公司), 1935-1936.

11. New Youth 新青年, Vol. 5, Ch. 4 (1918).

12. Tian, Ben Xiang (田本相), *Comparative Study of Modern Drama History in China* (中國現代比較戲劇史), Culture and Art Publish Company (文化艺术出版社), 1993.

13. Tian, Ben Xiang (田本相), *Comparative Study* 1993, P. 273

Chapter Six

Some Thoughts after the Show of *Peony Pavilion*

ON KUNQU (昆曲) AND JINGJU (京劇)

Kunqu (昆曲) or Kun Drama rose and reached its Golden Age from the mid-Ming period to the beginning of the Qing (清朝) (1644–1911 AD). For almost four hundred years, it dominated the stage of Chinese performing arts. Like many literary genres, its classic beauty, lyrics, and acting slowly attract less and less among the commoners in the mid of Qing Dynasty. Kun drama retired to the elite households and remained more and more as a literary art for intellectuals. At the same time, Jingju (京劇) or Beijing Opera gradually evolved out of several local dramas and singing tones into today's national theatre. In answering the need of stage entertainment for the public, these local tones were generally called Luan Tan (亂彈) with singing verses that were rather coarse and vulgar. As they combined and merged with the tone of Hui Oiang (徽腔) and finally evolved as Beijing opera (京劇), some of their folk characteristics were inherited. Therefore, compared with Kun drama, Beijing opera was never intended to be as elegant and refined in literary style. If we examine the lyrics, the rhetoric and rhyme structure are of a much different level. Lyrics in Kun drama are profound and precise in following the rule of Ci or Qu's formats (詞牌or曲牌), whereas in Beijing opera, the singing verses are not composed with any lyric format. Lyrics in Kun drama are literature and can be taught in academic institutions with Tang poetry (唐詩) and Song lyrics (宋詞). But singing verses in Beijing opera are not in the high style of literary works, even though they sound classic for today's audiences. They are loosely composed with some classic expressions mixed in vernacular dialogues and written in a hasty manner to appeal to popular taste. However, some of today's Beijing opera have inherited part of the dramatic acting and singing of Kun drama and should be considered exceptions, such as the *Visiting of Garden* (遊園) scene in *The Romance of the West Chamber* (西廂記) played by Cui Ying-ying (崔鶯鶯) and Hong Niang (紅娘), which is a copy of *Surprised in Dreamland* (遊園驚夢) in *Peony Pavilion* with Du Li Niang (杜麗娘) and Chun Xiang (春香). In these Beijing opera cases, the literary composition may be quite classical.

ON PROFESSOR BAI XIAN-YONG (白先勇)'S MODERN VERSION OF *PEONY PAVILION*

A background discussion of a classical drama and its modern features can enrich the understanding of readers. Professor Bai Xian-Yong (白先勇)'s modern version of *Peony Pavilion* retained all the original lyrics and singing but elaborated tremendously the acting and setting of the play. He made use of modern techniques and Western dramatic effects to embellish and flower his modern version. With magnificent costumes and a full orchestra of an expanded number of music instruments, the presentation is much more grandiose than the *Peony Pavilion* of Ming or Qing times. For instance, the audience is amazed to watch the use of the long red train of a cape to end the last act of the first part. It is quite bold for some Chinese, but a powerful way to modernize a dramatic scene. The expressions in a love scene using sleeves and eye contact, even slight shoulder touching, are choreographed to revive and recreate the sophisticated style of Kun drama. Beijing opera, even today, has never developed the kind of dancing-like steps and elegant sleeve expressions, "mingling, gathering, separating," as we have seen in his modernized *Peony Pavilion*. But Professor Bai proficiently adopts many acts and scenes of acrobatics that are popularly performed in today's Beijing opera. For example, the procession of the underworld judge entering on stage is characterized by Western dancing-like steps mixed with Beijing opera's acrobatics and style of dialogue. His application of a modern dance style develops complex and yet graceful actions. The many dancing scenes with a large group of ravishingly dressed girls splendidly ornament the play. Considering that Kun drama emphasizes lyrics and singing, this modern version of *Peony Pavilion* is really elaborated and amplified to compete on today's international drama stage.

Originally, Kun drama, like Western classical opera, emphasizes singing more than acting or complicated stage effects. In fact, dramatic effect included the appreciation of the literary composition of lyrics. At the end of its four hundred years life, Kun drama was reduced to singing with one flute only as an accompanist. Before Professor Bai's modernized version, many Kun drama clubs liked to perform the beginning scene of *Peony Pavilion*, *Surprised in Dreamland While Visiting the Garden* (遊園驚夢). It was usually performed with one major role, Du Li Niang (杜麗娘), singing with simple hand and sleeve gestures and accompanied with a flute only. Bai's elaborated play enormously lifted the face of the lost art, Kun drama with a whole troupe of performers.

ON THE DEATH AND REVIVAL OF LI-NIANG

Li-Niang (麗娘), the leading female role, had a dream of love-making with a young man. She became weak and slowly died afterwards. Questions often are asked where Li-Niang got the knowledge of love making. Speculation could be that, as a mature teenage girl, Li-Niang's physical development naturally prompts her longing for something mysterious, such as the male gender. Any gossip or hints talking among household maids about sex might strike the sensitive nerve of a lonely young girl. Therefore, what she heard or see could certainly lead her to have a dream of such. It seems that the author schemes with a tricky plan. Because she really should not have the knowledge of love-making, Tang Xian-zu (湯顯祖) should stop short her dream purposely by the sudden falling of flowers. But what about Li-Niang's slow death led by this dream? For modern audiences, how could it be possible that a dream would lead to death? If we hypothetically speculate from a modern-day point of view, it is the same design with flowers that could mentally shock Li-Niang and cause her to suffer post-traumatic stress. Brought up in a conservative household, psychologically Li-Niang could feel very guilty about "intimate" relations with a young man, even in her dream. This deranged mental depression plus her longing for Liu could contribute to the weakening of Li-Niang's already fragile physical condition and thus finally cause her to die. Many Chinese classic novels deal with this kind of "love sickness (相思病)."

During the dramatist Tang Xian-zu's (湯顯祖) lifetime, the religious practice of Buddhism and Taoism went to an extreme among the intellectuals. Obviously, he wants to emphasize that longing for loved ones could end a person's life; his whole dramatic narrative is based on this. He applied plenty of religious ideals in the drama. The mysterious dreams of both Li-Niang and Liu Meng Mai (柳夢梅), the leading male role, and the resurrection of Li-Niang and her romance with Liu before she was pardoned to be alive again are dotted with a mixture of the prophesies of the two religions. The chilling night scene when Li-Niang returns home is quite realistically modified, but it is a typical example in many Chinese ghost stories—folk Buddhist and Taoist traditions.

THE AUTHOR AND HIS "PHILOSOPHY OF EMOTION (情)"

Tang Xian-zu was brought up in an elite family to be public officials like millions of Chinese intellectuals in Chinese history. His life supposedly proceeded quite successfully in public service considering his literary talent. However, like most of the great novelists and dramatists of the Yuan-Ming era, he was a frustrated member of the literati who achieved mediocre success in the Civil Examination. He did not pass the Imperial Court level of examination till 1583, thirteen years after his success on the provincial level examination at age 21 in 1570. Actually, it was not because he was less qualified or talented, but a result of corrupted practices in the imperial court. His failure partially was due to his resistance of taking the favorite arrangement of the then Prime minister. As always, those who held lofty moral standards and self-assertiveness would not give in to their personal principles to join the hegemonic group ascending up the ladder of social mobility. His final success on the examination did not reward him with a high official position. In addition, he had, at one time, annoyed the emperor by submitting a memo attacking the corruption of powerful court officials. His advice grants him fame, but results in demotion. His loyalty to the country and sincere advice was not appreciated. Disappointed and frustrated, Tang lost his sincerity-seeking public life and ended his career quite early. Nevertheless, positions that he held and retired from, though of a local mediocre level, credited him with being a beloved official.

As usually happened to prominent scholar-officials in China, Tang left us his literary achievements. His talent and accomplishment in music and lyrics superseded his political life. It is interesting to know that his great plays were the result of his rebellion against the mainstream intellectual thought of his time. At the end of the Ming era, the inspirational Neo-Confucian school (宋明理學) completed its exertion. The lack of fresh thinking and rigid indoctrination in ethical social codes (禮教) went together with the decline of the dynasty. The Confucian trend of thought, to the time of Tang, lost its creative spirit that originated in the beginning of Ming time by Wang Yang-ming (王陽明) and his followers. The overly dogmatic interpretation of Confucian classics by late Ming scholars intended to dominate peoples' thinking and suffocated the free spirit of many intellectuals. The enforcement of family living by setting rules for women according to the ethical codes (禮教) was worse than ever in Chinese history. It was later criticized as too strict to limit expressions of natural desires and thus went against human nature.

Free spirit intellectuals, or "Reactionary scholars," such as Li Zhi (李贄) and Luo Ru-fang (羅汝芳) rose to oppose the conservatives and advocated Dao of natural expressions. They propelled the philosophy that the Tao (道) existed in all facets of people's daily life, eating, drinking, even sex. They cherished true individual expression and wanted to break free from the philosophical outlook of ancient sages and their classics. Tang was a great admirer of Li Zhi and Luo Ru Fang and joined to criticize the spurious and ignorant doctrines of conservatism and promoted absolute liberation for women from the bondage of orthodox ethical codes. On literary style, Tang also found that the effort to revive classic literary writing by conservative scholars was insignificant. All these philosophical disputes influenced him and resulted in his belief in the primacy of "emotion or passion情" and intense interest in writing about it.

It was said that he proclaimed that "sentiment or passion 情" is the driving force of literature. For delivering one' "sentiment 情," poetry or drama was written. All human being are born with this feeling whose original nature should be retained not suffocated. He believed that "true sentiment or passion 至情" loftily stands above the "reasoning or principle理" promoted by the then School of Principle (理學) as the doctrine for the investigation. Tang argued that this true "sentiment 情" cannot exist together with the principle (理), to search for the meaning or value of things, harmoniously. When the principle (理) directs the subject and transcends the mind, "sentiment or passion情" becomes oppressed or twisted. Accordingly, when sentiment (情) rises, principle (理) has to diminish. His dedication as a playwright and lyrical composer in the later days of his life was genuinely found in his philosophy of this sentiment or love (情). The cherishing of this sentimnt (情) became the core issue of his dramas. He remarked that human nature cannot be defined as good or evil, but "sentiment or passion情" can. Good intentioned sentiment (情) is most worthy to be treasured. Nothing in the human world is trustworthy and beautiful but "true sentiment or passion 至情." True love can transcend life and death. He often uses dreams to illustrate his belief. For instance, Lui Meng-Mei's dream in the garden led to the death and resurrection of Hui Niang. The love affair carried out between a human (Liu) and a spirit (Hui Niang) also authenticates this phenomenon.

The worth and quality of a drama, according to Tang, depends on how sincere the true sentiment (至情)" is involved in the story. "Love愛情" in drama, he commended, if it is "true sentiment情" between a man and woman in pursuing a happy life, ratifies a good drama. Those dramas that deal with scenarios seeking fame or wealth and threaded with "evil love or emotion" are bad plays. It is based on his interpretation on drama with "true or evil sentiment " that the love affair in *Peony Pavilion* was written. He designated his story to show how Li Niang and Liu Meng-mei's "true love情" eventually satisfied the pursuit of happy married life. Interestingly to observe, when he made the Judge in Hell to excuse Li-Niang from death, his strong ethical values stand out. The sole testimony that the judgment was based on was that Li-Niang was still a virgin. Her loss of innocence had taken place in a dream, not in reality.

It seems that Tang's so-called "true love情" is righteously within his ethical values. In view of his life experience, he was not sarcastically frustrated like Guan Han (關漢卿) who drowned himself among prostitutes. Those who were close to Tang were all serious scholars. Tang had a very strong moral judgment—to ease the bad and promote the good (抑惡揚善).

Chapter Seven

Chinese Comic Literature

Discussion of A Witty Short Story

Comicality and wittiness are qualities of behavior and speech, and comedy is a form of drama characterized by such behavior and speech. Comic literature—as distinguished from farces or comic strips—relies on wit to be amusing and humorous. It should arouse the readers' mirth either by means of episodes containing coincidental and unexpected circumstances or by means of witty characters. Although comic literature is not a well-established category in classical Chinese literature, a chapter dealing with this topic may be of some interest. Two classic Chinese novels have achieved renown for their unique humor and may undoubtedly be defined as the best representatives of comic Chinese literature. These are the *Journey to the West* (西遊記) and *The Scholars* (儒林外史), both of which display a profound sense of humor, and have been praised, studied, and introduced to non-Chinese readers by numerous scholars.

Journey to the West contains two of the elements that make up comic literature—a witty character in the lead role and ingeniously crafted episodes. The Monkey amuses people with both his clever handling of all kinds of precarious situations, and with his witty dialogue. The episodes in this novel are memorable for their amazing imaginativeness and metaphorical significance. The other Chinese novel, *The Scholars*, is a satirical novel that lampoons and ridicules the Chinese civil examination system in imperial times and is also an excellent piece of comic literature. Its comicality does not stem from the subjective actions of any of the characters, but rather from the content and circumstances of the episodes. The trenchant descriptions of aspiring scholars' stale and idiotic life styles and their adherence to absurd scholar-gentry convention triggers derision and laughter. However, since both of these lengthy novels have been so thoroughly studied and discussed by other scholars, this chapter will not repeat their efforts.

The refined classical writings by seriously-minded and erudite scholar officials in former days generally consisted of works of poetry, prose, essays, memoirs, letters, and memorials for the imperial court, and provided no occasion for describing witty characters with lively behavior and earthy humor. During the entire period of the Ming and Qing dynasties, novels of highbrow literary quality built around one witty character were scarce, apart from the afore-mentioned Monkey. But among the short vernacular stories and tales, a few were ingeniously plotted and centered on a variety of "unorthodox" characters of considerable wit and verve.

To find comic characters for the discussion of comic literature, one must search through novels and short stories of lesser prestige and lesser "snob" value. Such novels and short stories were written for the most part by writers who had been rejected by the civil service examinations. Although spurned by the scholarly elite, most of these leisure writings are excellent literature in the vernacular style and enjoyed a much delayed fame after their death. One successful example is *The Ingenious Judgment of Magistrate Qiao* (喬太守亂點鴛鴦譜),[1] a tale that fits admirably in the category of witty and comic literature. It is one of forty short stories in the *Fantastic Tales New and Old* (今古奇觀), a set of fifty tales selected from more than two hundred in the collection entitled *Three Tales and Two Slaps* (三言二拍).[2] This tale's ingenious plot dramatizes both the caustic wit and strong tendency toward civil libertarianism on the part of a local administrator.

At the end of the Ming Dynasty, these stories were written in the vernacular but as refined literary versions of the Song Dynasty storytellers' tales. Although these stories had more elaborate plots, they shared and retained the essential features of the original Song oral recitals. The episodes were usually treated in a realistic and earthy manner, with the events strung together one after the other. In addition to rendering moral messages and relating the usual love affairs between literary scholars and their ladies, these stories depicted a very broad spectrum of the social classes of those days. By the standards of the literary elite, the language in which these stories were written out was regarded as crude and of little literary merit. However, with their readers—mostly commoners—these works were immensely popular for their "excellent descriptions of society and manners, joy and sorrow, separations and reunions"[3] of a wide range of people in mostly urban settings. For this reason, these stories provide an incredible amount of information that is worthy of examination in order to gain an understanding of Chinese social traditions.

A BRIEF ACCOUNT OF *THE INGENIOUS JUDGMENT OF MAGISTRATE QIAO* (喬太守亂點鴛鴦譜)

A dispute among three families over a complicated topsy-turvy set of marriage arrangements is the chaotic case that Judge Qiao was called on to resolve. It involves the love, happiness, and wellbeing of three young people. A family surnamed Liu in the city of Hong Chou has two children and the older one, a boy named Liu Pu, is engaged to be married to Zhu Yi, the daughter of widow Sun in the same city. When Liu Pu is sixteen, a proposal to wed the young couple is sent to widow Sun. Unfortunately, Liu Pu falls gravely ill as the wedding day approaches. Hoping that the "event of great joy" will drive Liu Pu's bad luck away and hasten his recovery, the Liu family conceals the truth and proceeds with the wedding plans. But news travels fast in the city. Apprised of the true situation by a neighbor, Widow Sun becomes extremely worried that her daughter might herself become a widow if Liu Pu does not get better. Out of desperation, she disguises her handsome son, Sun Run, as the bride and sends him to the wedding, but not before securing a promise to have the "bride" sent home after three days, whether or not the groom's condition improved or worsened.

Covered with a headdress and heavy wedding gown, the boy looks strikingly beautiful and is presented without arousing any suspicion. Making an excuse for the absence for her son, Mrs. Liu has her beautiful fifteen-years-old daughter, Hui Niang, take the place of her son during the ceremony. Ignorant of Widow Sun's conspiracy, she insists that the young girl accompany the lonely "bride," Sun Run, on the wedding night and subsequent nights while the gravely ill bridegroom sleeps in a separate room. Three days had soon passed. The "bride" is persuaded not to go home, and the young couple meanwhile becomes helplessly infatuated with one another and deeply involved in their sweet affection.

The deceit inevitably comes to light, and the scandalous revelations electrify the Liu family and ignite explosive anger in the Liu household. Accusations fly not only between the Lius and the Suns, but also from the Feis, whose son has long been engaged to Hui Niang. The Liu family holds Widow Sun responsible for their daughter's ruined prospects of marriage into the prominent Fei family. Seeking compensation for Hui Niang's loss of virginity to Sun Run's reprehensible behavior becomes the paramount concern of the Lius. Widow Sun in turn accuses the Liu family of covering up the truth of Liu Pu's illness which forced her to resort to the deceit. Meanwhile, the Fei family lodges a complaint denouncing the Liu family's disreputable handling of the matter which has destroyed their son's marriage, and in turn demands the repayment of the money previously paid for their son's betrothal.

When the chaotic case finally reaches the court of the Magistrate Qiao, the dispute centers on which family should be held responsible for the monetary compensation for the confused course of events surrounding the respective marriage arrangements. The contempt and indignation over the scandalous relationship between Hui Niang and Sun Run trigger tremendous outbursts of emotion from all parties.

Aware of the awkwardness and intricacy of the situation at a time when marriage is mostly arranged by the family and when a woman's chastity is highly valued and guarded by a strict code of ethics, Magistrate Qiao makes an unorthodox but ingenious judgment. No preponderance of evidence is requested, nor does heated debate take place during the proceedings of the court. His judgment was as follows:

1. Both the Suns and the Lius are faulted for the scandalous arrangements during the wedding proceedings. Since it is understandable that the awkward situation arose because of the parents' love for and protection of their children, no punishment is imposed. However, Sun Run and Hui Niang should be wedded, for they were the helpless victims of alleged misconduct by their families.
2. Lu Pu's marriage to Zhu Yi (Sun Run's sister) is to be legally recognized and consummated, since Lu Pu has recovered from his illness.
3. Sun Run's long engaged fiancée, Xu Ya, is also summoned to the court. To compensate the Fei family for its loss, Magistrate Qiao rules that the Xus' daughter is to be wedded to the son of the Fei family.

The quarrel is thus settled at the discretion of the Magistrate Qiao whose match of the three young couples is described as genius deed and brilliant solution for a felicitous marriage arrangement which satisfies all and allays the anger of the parents. All three families are said to be content with the settlement for which Magistrate Qiao gains great fame. The Liu family's neighbor who has attempted to sow discord and stir up ill-will between the two families feels so ashamed that she finally moves out of the county. According to the narration, Magistrate Qiao's adroit handling of the awkward family quarrel is greatly admired by every household in the district of Hang Zhou. This cleverly dramatized civil case sensitively presented and realistically reflects the social customs for arranging marriages and the ethics related to a girl's virginity.

THE COMIC CHARACTER OF THE NARRATIVE

There is no question that the complexity of the narration provides the essential framework for making this tale a gem of comic literature and through which the comic and witty effects are crafted. Unlike most of the stories in the San Yen (三言) collection, this tale departs from the usual moral admonitions and ends with an unconventional judgment that is witty in its own way. The story does not contain ludicrous or clownish descriptions designed to draw ribald laughter. The humor is conveyed by a plot that centers on the serious venture of arranging marriages for offspring in a society where family relationships carry weighty importance.

From the beginning, tragic events overshadow the entire story, with each stage of development taking a surprising turn. Yet all events are tightly developed in a natural sequence that yields to dramatic developments. At each step, new problems are raised for which there seems to be no alternative. Emotions become ever tenser. Widow Sun's decision to disguise her son as the bride first takes readers by surprise and foreshadows the comedic nature of the tale. This novel arrangement leads to the inevitable wedding night events. Although the intentions were to conceal Mother Liu's selfish action, they result in a shockingly shameful family scandal. One after another, the actions taken by the parents were well-thought and meticulously planned for the sake of remedying what might have turned out to be a tragic marriage. Unfortunately, all their decisions seem to lead to miserable outcomes for their children. Although the urgency to resolve the vexing case intensifies tragically step by step, genuine wittiness prevails. While readers speculate and worry, the plot unfolds with more surprise developments.

As the story reaches its climax and leaves the readers pondering solutions, the tragic confusion ends up in court with all parties angry at each other and feeling mistreated. It would seem at first sight that the entangled engagement and love affair among the young couples and their families' quarrels are impossible to resolve. Chances for a satisfactory settlement for any or all parties involved look unlikely. But, unexpectedly, the clever Magistrate Qiao skillfully resolves the tangled affair and converts the seemingly irreconcilable happenings into a win-win solution. The Magistrate's sharp-witted and unconventional decision solves all the problems and makes every party happy. The unexpected ending startles everybody. Readers take delight as the wit and comedy of the tale come full circle. The cleverly crafted happy ending amazes and amuses readers with its incomparable ingenuity—an ending that is unorthodox yet still satisfies traditional moral doctrines. The work is a triumph for the narrator.

The whole scheme orchestrated by Mother Liu creates the involuntary circumstance for her daughter to commit adultery. It is another comic treatment. The author depicts a picture of the stunned Mother Liu facing a completely unanticipated development—the affection between Hui Niang and Sun Run. Her embarrassment and self-inflicted retribution reward the readers with some feelings of justice and ironic humor. The pity of it is that the incident does waken her awareness of the possible danger to the future of the two innocent young people—of the cruelty of the public contempt that her daughter would have to endure.

Instead of quietly negotiating with Widow Sun for a possible solution to the helpless situation, to the readers' astonishment, Mother Liu raises the case publicly in court and laments over her financial lost. All her actions, from her senseless and selfish proposal for her sick son's wedding to her suing the Sun's over her daughter's loss of virginity pitifully reveals how ignorant and imprudent she is. Her foolish personality is sketched so poignantly that one can hardly fail to find many like hers in real life. Another humorous scene consists of the unrestrained emotions displayed by the adults as they accuse one another of botching the marriage. If not for the clever judgment by Magistrate Qiao, Mother Liu's action could have brought grief to many people.

THE INGENIOUS JUDGMENT

For the sake of creating contrast, the author populates his tale with a number of conventional minded country folks versus a liberal judge. The parents, who muddle-mindedly stick to the social codes of ethics provide a contrast to point up Magistrate Chao's exceptional intelligence and his witty judgment. Recognizing the senselessness of their arguments, Magistrate Qiao ignores the parents' pleas and redirects their concern from their family reputation and financial debts to the future of the young couple. He tactfully admonishes the elders' foolishness that abetted the conduct of Hui Nian and Sun Run and successfully appeals to their instinctive parental affection, thereby skirting the rigid code that calls for punishing youngsters for premarital sex before consent is given for them to marry. As a consequence, he gains ground to swiftly confirm their helpless affection and remains pleasant, unruffled. He sagaciously departs from traditional ways and brings the case to a close without delivering any moralizing lectures.

His quick decision, which seems almost lighthearted at first sight, is actually quite thoughtful and based on his deep concern over the fate of Hui Niang. In reality, the behavior of Sun Run and Hui Niang could have had tragic effects on the young girl's life. The shame she brings to the family, as judged by the restrictive social codes of the time, would leave her no alternative other than suicide. If the case had been adjudicated in the traditional manner, the family would not only have had to honor the debt of the betrothal money paid by the Feis, but they would also have to cope with the grievous fate of their beloved daughter. Magistrate Qiao's kind concern deftly turns the tragic circumstances into a happy ending which extricates the Liu family from its dilemma and marries off their daughter in proper fashion.

With the main issue regarding Sun Run and Hui Niang being settled, Magistrate Qiao as a matter of course gives his consent to the marriage of the sick boy, Liu Pu, to the Suns' daughter. But the loose ends of the case are happily tied up only when he matches the Fei boy with Sun Run's fiancé and thereby assures a fortunate outcome for the hitherto unknown fate of these two young people. Most genuinely, by making this judgment he also frees himself from the necessity of pressuring any family into discharging financial responsibility. As the quarrel is settled and anger turns into happiness, the reaction of the readers is relief over the obviating of possible punishments for the transgressions innocently committed by Sun Run and Hui Niang. The author has given us an artfully crafted and vivid image of a genuine judge capable of unorthodox and quick, clever decisions. Magistrate Qiao's verdict leaves readers with a sense of justice done.

Readers' adoration for Magistrate Qiao was further enhanced by some remarkable interludes. On several reprises, the author ardently dwells on the exceptional beauty of Hui Niang and handsomeness of Sun Run, which at once come to Magistrate Qiao notice and arouse his sympathetic admiration. His memo testifies to his feelings and culminates in bringing the entire story to a high-flown conclusion.

His verdict reads: "The brother appeared at the wedding in his sister's stead, and the sister-in-law shared the bride's bed. These dispositions were not, in themselves, reprehensible, as they sprang from the parents' love for their children. However, the unexpected happened when the bride turned out to be a man. Dry wood, placed next to a blazing fire, will burst into flames.... The Sun's son found a wife through his sister; he needed not to climb over any walls to embrace the virgin. The Lius' daughter thought the man to be her sister-in-law; she did not seduce him with flirtatious advances. Happy with each other, they became a couple. True sentiments led to new commitments, and previous betrothals were forsaken. However, compromises had now been devised. Xu Ya has been enjoined to renounce her fiancé Sun Ruen. Pei Zheng, the son of Pei Jiu, will instead marry Sun Ruen's bride-to-be. Thus the resentments kindled between the three families will be laid to rest...."[4]

He mentions in particular that the match between Hui Niang and Sun Ruen is like pairing a piece of jade with a bright pearl—they are not a guilty couple. To justify his decision, he interjects many caustic remarks. Almost jocularly, he states that to have three happily matched couples is better than to have only one (couple). And since Sun Run has stolen someone else's betrothed, his should be stolen as well. He offers a rational solution by stating that even though the partners in three couples have been interchanged, in essence, things remain the same (as regards the number of people) anyway, just as one pound (jin斤) is equal to 16 ounces (liang兩). He declares that time will prove the matches are satisfactory. He ends his memo with the assertion that for the love of their children, the parents have unwittingly tightened the wedding knots for their children and that as a Magistrate—although not a relative—he is glad to have served as matchmaker for the young people.

Heavens! What an original and wryly humorous verdict the author has devised for the judge! The celebratory and merciful tone is astonishingly funny and certainly underscores the sensation of wittiness. Mostly of all, Magistrate Qiao's actions bear out the cleverness of his judgment and fascinate the reader with their unexpectedness. A witty character is at his best when he does not moralize but instead leads readers to enlightenment with the unfolding of surprise events. The wise settlement by Magistrate Qiao is a fascinating example that comical effect is produced by the quick wits of a major player. His expedient manner of unraveling a tangled and apparently hopeless situation and thus averting the aggravation of grievance achieves the best comic result.

HUMANITARIANISM AND UNORTHODOXY

When Feng Meng Lung wrote his collection of short stories at the end of the Ming period, Chinese society had just experienced a rejuvenation of tradition with the Neo-Confucian movement. To blend the Buddhist and Taoist elements into mainstream Confucianism, the Song- Ming scholars' philosophical investigations focused on the rationalization of mind.

This movement also gave rise to a renewed interpretation of the Confucian classics. Ethical guidelines for the common people's behavior had to conform to Confucian moral principles. Unfortunately, the social codes were particularly strict for women. Pressure from family members and public opinion forced widows to remain chaste. Women's virginity was required to satisfy the pleasure and standards of males. Methods for ascertaining a woman's virginity are described in many Ming era stories. The social stigma accruing from the shame of lost virginity is vividly dramatized by Hui Niang's vow to commit suicide.

Also, we learn how pitiful and helpless were those young girls who had to comply with the foolish custom of marrying a fiancé who is gravely ill like as was insisted on selfishly by Mother Liu. Yet, what she did was not an exceptional way of trying to save a sick son. It was customarily practiced by many people in that malecentered society.

But not to be overlooked is the belief then that a sick bridegroom bodes misfortune for any young girl and much more so for the daughter of a widowed parent. Widow Sun had good reason for not going along with the wedding plan. However, as a widow of moderate status in the community bound by the rules of the marriage agreement, she has to suppress her fears for her daughter's future. In desperation, then, she sends her young son disguised as the bride to the marriage ceremony.

What Magistrate Qiao breaks through is this web of commonly practiced Li Jiao (禮教), or the traditional Confucian code of ethics, also the standards set by Neo-Confucian scholars. He chooses to fulfill his role as a public official without exercising absolute adherence to the commonly practiced Li Jiao (禮教). Instead of reproving and blaming the youngsters, as most bureaucratic pedants of those days would probably have done, he condones their affection and gives his consent for marriage. However, to resolve an awkward and intricate situation at a time when marriage was mostly family-arranged and sealed by financial agreement, Magistrate Qiao has to resort to an unorthodox strategy. He passes a rare judgment filled with a humanitarian spirit and profound insights on the entangled relationship.

You may say that the author was indeed "treading on risky ground" when he created a clever judge to cut away the deadwood of social customs and resolve the case in a way that bypassed long entrenched strictures on behavior. In Magistrate Qiao's time, any relaxation of the rigid customary moral codes for settling problems in real life would win little applause. In fact, one could be severely criticized by his peers and forced to hand in his resignation.

It took wisdom, courage, and creativity to flout the social web of the times. The judge's decision gave people an alternative perspective which could inspire some people to stop parroting what was most believed. His unorthodox interpretation of the rules and his way of handling public affairs won widespread acclamation because people were becoming tired of being preached at and being dogmatically restrained by rigid rules. The judge's wit and the well-conceived and surprising happy ending are unorthodox but still fall within the norms of the Confucian moral doctrines.

Even though the Neo-Confucianism dominated the scene of the Song-Ming intellectual thought, the Taoist philosophical ideas is still quite alive among the educated. The attitudes promoted by Taoism, unlike the ethical codes of the Confucian school, more realistically follow the natural course of human life. The thought is reflected in the unorthodox astuteness of Magistrate Qiao. His witty character is a manifestation of the free spirit that Zhuan Zi (莊子) advocated. As the most influential interpreter of Taoist thought in ancient China, Zhuan Zi employed fables and metaphorical stories to humorously or trenchantly expound the law of nature of Taoism. As an intellectual the author understood the essence of many schools of thought. This he embodies in the judge—Magistrate Qiao—who wisely applied the spirit of the Taoists and Confucians to everyday life situations.

CONCLUSION

The best comic literature surprises readers with ingenious plots replete with coincidences mixed in with apparently unsolvable circumstances. Feng Meng long's tale, recounting a topsy-turvy and chaotic marriage dispute between three families, is one of the finest examples of comic literature. Central to the ironic comedy of the story is the witty character of Magistrate Qiao. The author skillfully presents the Magistrate's incomparable wit and sagacity in a relaxed and humorous ambience that belies the wisdom of Qiao's judgment on what is in reality a serious conflict. His judgment spares people from the turmoil and suffering likely to have accompanied application of the social practices of the times.

The surprise ending relaxes the tense emotions that have been painstakingly built up and implanted in the reader's mind. The originality of Magistrate Qiao's wit is abundantly evident in the ironically humorous statements of his final judgment, i.e. pairing jade with pearl, placing dry woods near a fire, etc.

While telling a totally engrossing and amusing story, Feng Menglong demonstrates a profound sense of humanity and a courageous spirit of unorthodoxy. This is a wisdom inspired by the teaching of Confucius, the compassion of Buddhism, and the natural Taoist approach to human affairs.

James Liu stated clearly in his *The Art of Chinese Poetry* that "Reading a poem in translation is like looking at a beautiful woman through a veil, or a landscape through a mist, of varying degrees of thickness according to the translator's skill and faithfulness. . . ." Teaching Chinese literature courses intended to give representation of major literary genres and works of chief literary components of some 2,500 years to people who have no or limited Chinese language ability and cultural knowledge is more challenging than teaching only poetry. In addition to the loss of beauty and flavor of original expressions through translation at times, the English wording also channels to the readers a visual domain of Western cultural settings instead of Eastern ones, which, in many cases, could cause misapprehension of the original work.

This chapter is a daring attempt to present a piece of Chinese literature demonstrating the comic sense of Chinese people.

NOTES

1. The tale was included in the collection of *Fantastic Tales New and Old* (今古奇觀), a set of forty short stories selected from more than two hundred tales of the Ming period from the *Three Tales and Two Slaps* (三言二拍). The Three Tales are *Instructive Tales to Enlighten the World* (喻世明言), *Popular Tales to Admonish the World* (警世通言), and *Lasting Tales to Waken the World* (醒世恆言). The Two Slaps are the first and second publications of the *Slapping the Desk in Astonishment* (拍案驚奇初刻及二刻).

2. The five short story collections of Ming Dynasty. The Three Tales, a collection of stories in three volumes, *Instructive Tales to Enlighten the World* (喻世明言), *Popular Tales to Admonish the World* (警世通言), and *Lasting Tales to Waken the World* (醒世恆言). *The Two Slaps* are the first and second publications of *Slapping the Desk in Astonishment* (初刻及二刻拍案驚奇).
3. Lu, Hsun, *A Brief History of Chinese Fiction*, West Point, Connecticut: Hyperion Press, 1959, 257.
4. Feng, Meng Long, *The Oil Vendor and the Courtesan: Tales from the Ming Dynasty*, trans. Ted Wang and Chen Chen. New York: Welcome Rain Publishers, 2006, 125–126.

Bibliography

史記, 滑稽列傳 [Shi ji, or *Biographies of the Witty*]. (Taiwan Commercial Press).
Bai, Xian Yong,白先勇. 青春版牡丹亭 [Modern Version Peony Pavilion] (2004).
Birch, Cyril ed., *Anthology of Chinese Literature: From Early Times to the Fourteenth Century*.
Feng, Meng Long. *The Oil Vendor and the Courtesan: Tales From the Ming Dynasty*, trans. Ted Wang and Chen Chen (New York: Welcome Rain Publishers, 2006), 125–126.
Hunt, Hugh. *The Abbey Ireland's National Theatre, 1904–1978,* New York: Columbia University Press, 1979).
Hu, Shi 胡適文集, 第二集 [Collected Essays of Hu Shi, Volume 2], ed. Ouyang Zhesheng (Beijing: Beijing University Press, 1998). Originally published in *New Youth* (October 1918) Volume 5, Number 4 (原載 新青年, 第五卷第四號, 1918 年10月).
Hu, Xing-Liang 胡星亮. 二十世紀中國戲劇思潮 [*Literary Trend of 20th Century Chinese Drama*].
Liu, Wu-chi, and Irving Yucheng Lo, *Sunflower Splendor: Three thousand Years of Chinese Poetry* (New York: Anchor Press/Doubleday, 1975).
Lu, Hsun. *A Brief History of Chinese Fiction*. (West Point, Connecticut: Hyperion Press, 1959).
Matthews, Brander. *The Development of the Drama* (New York: Charles Scribner's Sons, 1912), 74.
New Youth 5, Ch. 4 (1918).
New Youth 4, Ch. 6 (1918).
Olson, Elder. *The Theory of Comedy* (Bloomington: Indiana University Press), 36.
Sima, Qian. *The Development of the Drama* (New York: Charles Scribner's Sons, 1912).
Schevill, Ferdinand. "The Society of the Italian Renaissance," in *The Civilization of the Renaissance*, ed. James Westfall Thompson et al. (New York: Frederick Ungar Publishing Co., 1959).
史記, 滑稽列傳 [Shi ji, or *Biographies of the Witty*]. (Taiwan Commercial Press).
Yu, Shang-Yuan, 余上沅. 國劇運動 [*National Theater Movement*]. (Shanghai: Shanghai Book Store, 1992).
Zhu, Guang-qian, 朱光潛. 悲劇心理學, 人民文學出版社 (1982).

Index

Advising Husband by Killing a Dog (殺狗勸夫), 19
Ai Mei Club (愛美劇), 43
Aristotle, 52–54, 57

Ba Jin, 44; *Autumn* (秋), 44; *Family* (家), 44; *Spring* (春), 44
Bai Pu (白朴), 25
Bai Xian-Yong (白先勇), 82
Beijing Opera, 11, 20, 21, 24, 27, 69–70, 74, 81; criticisms of, 71; debate over, 63–64, 67; limitations of, 38, 73; presentation and format of, 20; proponents of conserving, 51, 74, 77; survival of, 78
Beijing Theatrical Arts Center (北京藝術劇院), 66
Beijing Theatrical Arts Institute (北京國立藝術專門學校), 74
Bloody Rain Coat (血蓑衣), 38
Buddhism, 13, 14, 61, 83

Cai Bo-jie (蔡伯喈), 10
Cai Yong (蔡邕) [also called Cai Bo-jie], 7, 8, 10
Cai Yuan-pei (蔡元培), 36
Cao Cao (曹操), 20; *The Lonely Journey of Guan Yu* (千里獨行), 20
Cao Xui-qing (曹雪芹), 18; *The Dream of the Red Chamber*, 61–62, 63

Cao Yu (曹禺) 44, 45, 46; *Sun Rise* (日出), 44, 46; *Thunderstorm* (雷雨), 44, 46; *Under the Roof in Shanghai* (上海屋簷下), 44
Chen Bao (晨報), 67
Chen Da-bei (陳大悲), 42, 43, 44; *The Hero and Beauty* (英雄與美人), 43; *Lady You Lan* (幽蘭夫人), 43
Chen Du-xiu (陳獨秀), 36, 45, 71, 76; *On Modern Literature and Traditional Chinese Drama* (新文學及中國舊戲), 72
Chen Shao-bai (陳少白), 41; *Zhen Tian Sheng Ju Tuan* (振天聲劇團), 41
Chinese drama: bittersweet tale genre, 18, 64; comedy in, 16, 55; debate over, 51, 63; "family soap-opera (家庭戲)" genre in, 39; "happy-family reunion (大團圓) settlement" in, 11, 22, 23; love and marriage as themes in, 23; as lower-class entertainment, 17, 50, 58; Ming Period, 7–12, 13, 19; modern stage play (文明戲) genre, 39–40, 44, 46, 47; moral teachings in, 13, 14, 15, 19, 20; novels in relation to, 18, 27, 28; poetry in, 24, 26, 28, 29; realism in, 44; representation of women in, 22, 24; social function of, 36, 45, 46; social status of, 16, 29; Song Period, 15, 16, 28, 88; Southern Melody, 9; Tang Period, 16, 28; theory of, 41, 44–45,

52–54; Yuan Period, 19, 24–26, 28
Chinese Drama Reform Club (中華戲劇改進社), 66
Chu Guang-qian (朱光潛), 63, 76, 77
College Press of Nan-Kai University (南開校風), 72
comedy: Chinese vs. Western definitions of, 16, 20, 29, 52, 57; Chinese comic literature, 87
Confucian elite-gentry, 15, 17, 51, 67
Confucianism, 13, 21, 24, 95

The Death of the Beloved Queen (此恨綿綿), 66
Ding Xi-lin (丁西林), 43; *A Bee* (一只蜜蜂) 43; *Oppress* (壓迫), 43

Eastern Magazine (東方雜誌), 45
Embroidered Robe (繡襦記), 23

The Fan of Yao Tao (夭桃紈扇), 23
Fang Chen (芳塵), 71
Feng Meng Lung, 94; *Fantastic Tales New and Old* (今古奇觀), 88; *The Ingenious Judgment of Magistrate Qiao* (喬太守亂點鴛鴦譜), 88, 89–94
The Firmiana Rain (梧桐雨), 23, 53
Fu Si-nian (傅斯年), 52, 76, 77, 79; *Again On Reform of Drama* (再論戲劇改良); *All Aspects of Drama Reform* (戲劇改良各面觀)

Gao Ze Cheng (高則誠) [also known as Gao Ming (高明)], 8–9, 18; *The Tale of the Lute* (琵琶記), 7–11, 19, 22, 58, 66
Gold and Blood (黃金赤血), 42
Green Mountain (青山記), 23
Gu Ta-dian (顧大典), 27; *Blue Robe* (青衫記), 27
Gu Yi-qiao (顧一樵), 66
Guan Han-qing (關漢卿), 18, 19, 24, 25, 26, 28, 86; *Pavilion of Wang Jiang Ting* (望江亭), 24; *Saved the Unfortunate Lady* (救風塵), 24; *Wu Hou's Dinner Party* (五侯宴), 19; *Xie Tian Xiang* (謝天香), 26
Guo Mo-ruo (郭沫若), 41, 43, 45, 46; *The Assassination of Xia Lei* (棠棣之花), 45; *The Phoenix* (孔雀膽), 46

Heroic Tales from the Water Margin (水滸傳), 14
Hong Shen (洪深), 42, 43, 45, 53, 77; *The Fan of the Fair Lady* (少奶奶的扇子), 42
Hong Sheng (洪昇), 27; *Palace of Longevity* (長生殿), 27, 56
Hu Shi (胡適), 43, 44, 45, 50, 66, 71, 76, 77, 79; *Marriage* (終身大事), 43; "The Progressive Concept of Literature and Reform of Drama (文學進化觀念與戲劇改良論)", 71

Ibsen, Henrik, 28, 40, 43, 44, 53, 54
The Injustice Done to Dou E (竇娥冤), 21, 25, 53, 58, 63, 77
Irish Theatre Movement, 66–67

Jia Zong-ming (賈仲名), 14; *Golden Young Couple* (金童玉女), 14
Jiang Guan-yun (蔣觀雲), 52
Jiang Zhao-xie (蔣兆燮), 72
The Jade Pin (荊釵記), 19
Jingju (京劇). *See* Beijing Opera

Kang You-wei (康有為), 36
Kong Shang-ren (孔上任), 27; *The Peach Fan* (桃花扇), 11, 27, 56
Kunqu drama [also known as Kun drama], 11, 56, 74–75, 79, 81

Lao She (老舍) [pen name of Shu Qing-chun], 46; *Tea House* (茶館), 46
Lee Hong-zhang (李鴻章), 35
Li Shou-qing (李壽卿), 18; *Lament for the Skeleton* (嘆骷髏), 18; *Wu Yuan Plays the Flute* (伍員吹簫), 20
Liang Chen-yu (梁辰魚), 27; *Clothes Washing* (浣紗記), 27
Liang Qi-chao (梁起超), 36, 43, 76; *Dream of Destruction* (劫灰夢), 36
Liang Shi-qiu (梁實秋), 66
Liang Si-cheng (梁思成), 66
Lin Hui-yin (林徽音), 66
Liu Ban-nong (劉半農), 52, 71, 76; *My Opinion on Literary Reform* (我的文學改良觀), 71
Liu Ya-zi (柳亞子), 45
Liu Yi-zhou (劉藝舟), 41

Index

The Loyal National Hero, Yue Fei (岳飛) (精忠記), 14, 19, 53
Lu Xun (魯迅), 41, 43, 45, 50, 76; *Wen hau pian zhi lun* (文化偏至論), 41

Ma Yan-xiang (馬彥祥), 53, 54, 59; *About Drama* (戲劇概論), 53
Ma Zhi-yuan (馬致遠), 24, 25, 26; *Autumn in Han Palace* (漢宮秋), 25, 27, 56; "Autumn Thought" (秋思), 24
Mao Dun (矛盾), 45
May Fourth Movement, 40, 42, 47, 50, 73, 78
Modern Chinese stage dramas, 74; similarity to Western dramas, 74; style of, 74
Morning Bell News (晨鐘報), 72
Mr. Ma Er (馬二先生), 71

Nan Kai Club (南社), 37, 47
National Beijing Arts Institute (北京國立藝術專門學校), 67
National Theatre Movement (國劇運動), 65–71
Neo-Confucianism, 10, 12, 95
New Moon Magazine (半月刊), 66
New Moon Press, 67
New People's Society (新民社), 39
New Wave (新潮), 45
New Youth group (新青年派), 68, 73, 77
New Youth Journal (新青年), 44, 45, 70, 71, 72
Novel Monthly (小說月報), 45

The Orphan Zhao (趙氏孤兒), 14, 56, 58, 60, 76

Ou Yang Yu-qian (歐陽予倩), 43; *My Opinion on the Reform of Drama* (予之戲劇改良觀), 72

Pei Du Returned the Jade Belt (裴度還帶), 19
Petition News (訟報), 72
The Political Scheme Using Diao Chan (貂蟬) in *Lian Huan Jin* (連環記), 19
The Progressive Society (進化團), 38, 39, 42
Public News (時事新報), 72

Public Opinion (公言報), 72
Puppet Magazine (傀儡雜誌), 66

Qi Ru-shan (齊如山), 74
Qian Xuan-tong (錢玄同), 52, 71, 76, 77, 79

Ren Tian-zhi (任天知), 38
Republican Daily, 45
Respect Always after Married (舉案齊眉), 19, 23
Reunion of the Immortal Couple (牛郎織女), 66
The Romance of the Eternal Palace (長生殿), 11
Romance of the Three Kingdoms (三國演義), 19, 27
The Romance of the West Chamber (西廂記), 11, 25, 28

The Scholars (儒林外史), 87
The Secret Volume at the Qin Palace (清宮秘史), 45
Shakespeare, William, 24, 28, 40–41, 53, 57, 66, 75
Shanghai People's Drama Club, 43
Shao Wen-ming (邵文明), 18
Shen Jing, 27; *Green Mountain Screen* (翠屏山), 27
Shen Shou-xian (沈受先), 14; *San Yuan Ji* (三元記), 14
Shi Na-an (施耐庵), 18
Sick Man in East Asia (東亞病夫), 38
Song Period (960–1279AD), 10
Song Chun-fang (宋春舫), 45, 54, 74; *An Introductory List of One Hundred European Dramas* (近世名戲百種目), 72
Spring Willow [press media] (春柳), 72
Spring Willow Club (春柳社), 37, 39, 41, 47, 66

Tan Si-tong (譚嗣同), 36
Tang Period (618–907AD), 10
Tang Xian-zu (湯顯祖), 18, 27, 84–86; biography of, 84; *Nan Ke Dream* (南柯記), 27; *Peony Pavilion* (牡丹亭), 11, 23, 27, 79, 82–83; philosophy of emotion (情), 85–86; *Resurrection* (還

魂記), 27
Taoism, 9, 13, 21, 23, 83
Three Tales and Two Slaps (三言二拍), 88
Tian Han (田漢), 40, 42, 43, 45
To Elope with Xiang Ru (私奔相如), 23
The Top Candidate Zhang Xie (張協狀元), 10, 23
Tragedy 20, 29, 30n11, 52–61

vernacular language movement, 50, 77
The Virtuous Lady Zhao and the Cai Er Long (赵贞女蔡二郎), 9

Wang Guo-wei (王國維), 56, 79
Wang Shi-pu (王實甫), 18, 25, 26, 28
Wang Zhong-wen (王仲文), 19; *Han Xin Begs for Food* (韓信乞食), 19
Wen Yi-duo (聞一多), 66, 67; "The Wrong Path of Traditional Drama (舊劇的歧途)", 67
Western Drama: debate over, 51; differences from Chinese drama, 20, 29, 36, 53, 56–60; influence of, 28, 35, 36, 37–38, 43, 50, 53, 54; introduction of, 37, 50; popularity of, 50; purpose of, 17; Renaissance period, 17, 20, 59; style of, 24; values in, 15
Western Literature : influence of, 42, 50, 52; introduction of, 40–41, 44, 50
White Rabbit (白兔記), 19
Wu Chang-ling (吳昌齡), 14; *Dream of Dong Po* (東坡夢), 18; *Merry Go Lucky* (風花雪月), 14; *The Tang Tripitaka's Journey Seeking Sutras to the West* (唐三藏西天取經), 14, 19, 27
Wu Cheng-en (吳承恩), 14, 18; *The Journey to the West* (西遊記), 14, 87
Wu Jing-zhi (吳敬梓), 18
Wu Wo-zhun (吳我尊), 42; *River Wu* (烏江), 42

Xiao Xiang Raining Night (瀟湘夜雨), 23
Xiong Fo-xi (熊佛西), 28, 53, 66, 77
Xu Ban-mei (徐半梅), 43
Xu Zhi-mo (徐志摩), 45, 66, 67; The Founding of Drama Journal (劇刊始業)

Xu Zi-shou (須子壽), 14; *The Bodhisattva Subjugates the Ocean Demon* (泗州大怪淹水母), 14

Ya Xian Saved Yuan He (亞仙助元和), 23
Yan Du-he (嚴獨鶴), 72
Yan Fu (嚴復), 36
Yao Mao-liang (姚茂良), 14, 18; *Loyalty* (精忠記), 14
Ye Xian-zhu (葉憲祖), 27; *Flowery Phoenix* (團花鳳), 27
Yu Shang-yuan (余上沅), 66, 67, 68, 74; "Evaluation of Traditional Drama (舊戲評價)", 67; "National Theatre Movement (國劇運動)", 67
Yun Tie-qiao (惲鐵樵), 72

Zhang Bo-ling (張伯苓) and Zhang Peng-chun (張彭春), 37, 52; *Awakening* (醒), 37–38; *Knowledge Failed in Reality World* (用非所學), 37–38
Zhang Feng-yi (張鳳翼), 27; *Homg Fo Romance* (紅拂記), 27
Zhang Geng (張庚), 54
Zhang Hou-zai (張厚載), 71, 72; *Modern Literature and Traditional Chinese Opera* (新文學及中國舊戲), 72; *My View on Traditional Chinese Opera* (我的中國舊戲觀), 72; *Painted Face and Acrobatics* (臉譜, 打把子), 72
Zhang Jia-chou (張嘉儔), 65
Zhang Min (章泯), 54
Zhao Tai-mou (趙太侔), 43, 66, 67, 68; "Classical Drama (國劇)", 67
Zhou Jian-yun (周劍雲), 74
Zhou Zuo-ren (周作人), 43, 72; *On the Abandonment of Traditional Drama* (周作人), 72; *Traditional Chinese Drama Should Be Abandoned* (中國舊戲之應廢), 72
Zhu Guang-qian (朱光潛), 28, 52, 76, 79; "Psychology of Tragedy" (悲劇心理學), 52
Zhuan Zi (莊子), 95

About the Author

Teresa Chi-Ching Sun has taught Chinese Cultural History at the University of California, Irvine; California State University at Los Angeles; and California State University at Long Beach. She is the author of *The Admission Dispute: Asian American Versus University of California at Berkeley*. She has a B.A. in Chinese literature from Taiwan Normal university.

www.ingramcontent.com/pod-product-compliance
Lightning Source LLC
Chambersburg PA
CBHW030118010526
44116CB00005B/305